Good News for KIDS

Series C

52 GOSPEL TALKS

Elizabeth Friedrich
Jane Wilke
Judy Christian and David Christian
Anita Reith Stohs

CPH®

Concordia Publishing House

Copyright © 1997 Concordia Publishing House
3558 S. Jefferson Avenue, St. Louis, MO 63118-3968
Manufactured in the United States of America

Library of Congress Cataloging-in-Publication Data

Good news for kids : 52 Gospel talks / Elizabeth Friedrich ... [et al.].
   p. cm.
   Contents: [1] Series C
   ISBN 0-570-04855-9 (Series):
   1. Bible—Liturgical lessons, English. 2. Christian education of children.
I. Friedrich, Elizabeth, 1949-
BS2565.G66   1995

252'.53—dc20   95-5762

---

1 2 3 4 5 6 7 8 9 10   06 05 04 03 02 01 00 99 98 97

Contents

Coming Once, Coming Twice

⋙⬩◆⬩⋘

FIRST SUNDAY IN ADVENT:
Luke 21:25–36

Text: At that time they will see the Son of Man coming in a cloud with power and great glory. When these things begin to take place, stand up and lift up your heads, because your redemption is drawing near. *Luke 21:27–28*

Teaching aids: A box wrapped in Christmas gift paper, a Christmas ornament, a cookbook, a Bible.

Gospel truth: Jesus promised to come back and take us to heaven to live with Him forever.

Hold up box wrapped in Christmas gift paper. Have you seen any boxes like this around your house lately? Maybe you and your mother or father have even unpacked some of these. *Hold up Christmas ornament.* Or, maybe someone has already been working hard in the kitchen to make special treats. *Hold up cookbook.*

This is a busy time of year. It's called Advent. The word *advent* means "coming." Who do you think is coming? *Let the children respond.* That's right, Jesus is coming. He's the reason we wrap the gifts and decorate the tree and bake the cookies. His coming is what Advent is all about.

The gifts and trees and cookies are all signs that tell us Jesus is coming. When we watch Father wrap a Christmas gift or help Grandma bake gingerbread or find just the right spot for our favorite ornament, we get excited because we know Christmas is coming. We know it's almost time for baby Jesus to be born.

Jesus came to earth as a tiny baby who grew up and helped many people. He loved us all so much that He even died on the cross to save us from our sins. But Jesus didn't stay dead, He came alive again! Now He's in heaven. *Hold up Bible.* In the Bible, Jesus promised to come to earth again. *Open Bible and read.* He said, "They will see the Son of Man coming in a cloud with power and great glory."

What exciting words those are! Jesus is coming again! And this time He won't be a tiny baby. He will come with power and glory. But the best part of all about Jesus coming again is that He promised to take us to heaven to be with Him. We will live forever in heaven with Jesus.

This Advent as you are wrapping gifts and decorating trees and baking goodies, remember Jesus came first at Christmas and someday He will come again to take us home with Him to heaven. What a happy, happy day that will be!

The Bible also tells us: *Open Bible and read Luke 21:27–28.* Let's all stand up and look up to heaven as we pray to Jesus together.

Prayer: Dear Jesus, thank You for coming to earth as a tiny baby on that first Christmas. Thank You for loving us so much that You died to save us from our sins. And thank You for promising to come again and take us to heaven to live with You forever. Amen.

Prepare the Way

——◆——

SECOND SUNDAY IN ADVENT:
Luke 3:1–6

Text: Prepare the way for the Lord, make straight paths for Him. *Luke 3:4*

Teaching aids: A broom, dusting cloth, furniture polish, bucket.

Gospel truth: God sent Jesus to be our Savior from sin. During Advent we prepare our hearts for His coming.

I brought some supplies with me today. *Hold up each item as it is mentioned.* When you see a broom, a dusting cloth, some furniture polish, and a bucket, what kind of work do you think I am going to do? *Let children respond.* That's right. I'm going to clean house. I'm cleaning the house because company is coming, and I want to make sure my house looks as nice as it possibly can for my guests. I'm going to sweep and dust and pick up clothes and take out old newspapers and do everything I can to prepare my house for my guests.

Isaiah, a prophet in the Old Testament, talked about someone who would prepare the way for Jesus. Isaiah said, "a voice of one calling in the desert" will "prepare the way for the Lord." Isaiah said because of this person "crooked roads shall become straight, the rough ways smooth" (Luke 3:4–5).

In Bible days there were not many paved roads like we have today. When a king was going to visit someplace, his servants built roads for him so that his chariot could travel safely and easily. They would prepare the way for their king.

When Jesus was ready to begin His ministry here on

earth, God sent a man called John the Baptist to prepare people for Jesus' message. That's the person Isaiah was talking about. John the Baptist lived in the desert. He wore clothing made of camel's hair, tied a leather belt around his waist, and put sandals on his feet. He ate wild honey and locusts. Locusts are insects like grasshoppers. You might not think grasshoppers are good to eat, but many people who lived in the desert ate insects all the time.

John the Baptist gave powerful sermons, and people traveled for miles to hear him preach. He told people to stop doing bad things and to ask God for forgiveness. He baptized people to help them get ready for Jesus the Savior.

The four weeks of Advent are a special time to prepare our hearts for Jesus' arrival. But sometimes during the weeks in Advent we get so busy with our Christmas preparations by shopping and baking and wrapping and decorating that we forget to prepare our hearts for Jesus' coming.

This week, stop and prepare your heart for Jesus. Write a Christmas poem or prayer. Read the Bible together. Assemble a nativity scene. Look at the stars and remember the special star God placed over the stable. Sing "Joy to the World." Fold your hands and say a prayer with me.

Prayer: Dear Jesus, this Advent I want to prepare my heart for You. I'm sorry for the times I do things I shouldn't do. And I'm sorry for the times I don't do things I should. Forgive me. Thank You for being my Savior. Amen.

Giving Hearts

⟹◦⟸

THIRD SUNDAY IN ADVENT:
Luke 3:7–18

Text: "What should we do then?" the crowd asked. John answered, "The man with two tunics should share with him who has none, and the one who has food should do the same." *Luke 3:10–11*

Teaching aids: Christmas list with two or three items; Christmas list with many items; tie; handmade gift; large cut-out paper heart; small hearts for each child; large cardboard box decorated with Christmas paper to fill with inexpensive gifts for those in need (for example: mittens for needy children or toothbrushes for people in a nursing home or canned foods for local food pantry).

Gospel truth: God loved us so much that He sent His own Son, Jesus, to save us from our sins. He will help us show His great love to everyone we meet.

Hold up short list. How many of you made a Christmas list this year of all the things you hoped to receive? *Let the children respond.* It sounds like some of you might have made a list more like this one. *Hold up long list.*

I think we all enjoy receiving gifts at Christmas. I know I do. Every gift I receive reminds me of the best Christmas gift of all—the gift that God gave us on that first Christmas—baby Jesus. Because Jesus came into the world as a tiny baby who grew up to die for us on the cross and rise again on the third day, we know we will live forever in heaven. That's an awesome gift!

Because God has given us such a wonderful gift in baby

Jesus, we like to give gifts too. It's fun to go to the store and pick out just the perfect tie for Dad. *Hold up a tie.* And it's even more fun when we work hard to make that perfect pottery bowl or that colorful potholder or our best painting ever for someone we love. *Hold up handmade gift.* Every time I give a gift at Christmas who do you think I remember? *Let children respond.* That's right! I remember baby Jesus, the best Christmas gift of all.

I'd like to read you a poem about a problem one boy had at Christmas. It goes like this:
I'm ready for Christmas. What more can I do?
I've worked and I've wrapped all these presents so new.
For Dad I've a picture of blue and green skis.
For Mother a jar filled with dirt and two leaves.
For Grandpa a yellow and pink painted rock.
And Sister gets bubble gum inside a sock.
There's something for everyone I love the best.
Except for Jesus! I remembered the rest.
What can I give Him? A balloon or a cart?
I know what I'll give Him. I'll give Him my heart.
(From *Happy Times,* copyright © 1989 Concordia Publishing House.)

Hold up cut-out paper heart. That boy gave Jesus his heart for Christmas. That means he loves Jesus. I'm going to give each of you a paper heart. You can write your name on the heart. Then during the offering, you can place the heart in the offering basket to show Jesus you love Him.

When our hearts are filled with love for Jesus, that love just bubbles over and we want to share it with everyone. One way we can share that love at Christmas is by giving gifts to people who need some help. *Hold up large decorated cardboard box.* This is our Giving Box. This week we are going to fill this box with [whatever gift you decided to collect] for [whoever the gift is for]. When you come to church next Sunday, bring a [name gift] with you and place it in the box. Let's share Jesus' love with everyone we can this Christmas!

Prayer: Dear God, thank You for giving us the best Christmas gift of all—Your Son, baby Jesus. We want to give our hearts as a gift to Jesus. Fill our hearts with so much love for Him that it bubbles over and touches everyone we meet. Amen.

Joy to the World

———◆———

FOURTH SUNDAY IN ADVENT:
Luke 1:39–45

Text: In a loud voice she exclaimed: "Blessed are you among women, and blessed is the child you will bear!" *Luke 1:42*

Teaching aids: Large sheet of poster board with the outline of a Christmas tree drawn on it and various colors of marking pens.

Gospel truth: God sent His Son, Jesus, to earth as a tiny baby. His birth fills our hearts with joy because we know Jesus is our Savior.

The Bible tells us that before Jesus was born, Mary, the mother of Jesus, went to visit Elizabeth, the mother of John the Baptist. The two women spent several months together preparing for the birth of Jesus. While she was visiting Elizabeth, Mary sang a beautiful song of praise to God. Both Mary and Elizabeth felt so happy because they knew Mary's baby was Jesus. And they knew Jesus would grow up to be their Savior from sin.

Christmas is a happy time for us too. The time we spend preparing for Jesus' birth fills us with anticipation and joy. One of my favorite preparations is decorating the Christmas tree. How many of you have a decorated Christmas tree at home? *Let the children respond.*

I brought a Christmas tree with me to church today, but I don't think it looks quite right. Here it is. *Hold up poster board with tree outline.* What's wrong with my Christmas tree? *Let the children give suggestions.* You're right. It needs ornaments. Let's put some ornaments on this tree.

Draw a star at the top of the tree. The star on the top of the Christmas tree reminds us of the bright star that God put into the sky the night Jesus was born. That star led the Wise Men to Jesus, and they brought Him gifts of gold and frankincense and myrrh.

Draw an angel outline on the tree. Angels announced the birth of Jesus. They sang "Glory to God in the highest" to shepherds sitting in the fields watching their sheep.

Draw candy canes on the tree. Candy canes remind us of the canes the shepherds carried when they came to worship baby Jesus.

This tree is looking more and more like a real Christmas tree. *Draw a few bell outlines on the tree.* Whenever I hear the happy sound of bells ringing at Christmas time, I think they are calling, "Jesus is born! Jesus is born!"

Draw small dots all over the tree. These are the sparkling lights on our Christmas tree. The lights remind us that Jesus lights up the whole world. He brings light into the darkness and brings hope into our lives.

Draw presents under the tree. The gifts underneath the tree remind us of the best Christmas gift of all. What do you think that is? *Let the children respond.* That's right. Baby Jesus! Jesus is the best gift of all. He is God's gift to us.

My tree looks much better now. It is filled with ornaments and decorations that remind me of Jesus. When you look at your tree at home, remember baby Jesus. Mary, the mother of Jesus, started singing beautiful songs when she thought about Him. Maybe you will too.

Prayer: Dear Jesus, whenever I think about Your birth, my heart is filled with joy. Thank You, Jesus, for coming to earth as a tiny baby. Thank You for loving me so much. Thank You for being my Savior. Amen.

Taller and Wiser

FIRST SUNDAY AFTER CHRISTMAS:
Luke 2:41–52

Texts: And Jesus grew in wisdom and stature, and in favor with God and men. *Luke 2:52*

"Didn't you know I had to be in My Father's house?" *Luke 2:49*

Teaching aids: Pair of baby shoes; larger child's pair of shoes; Bible.

Gospel truth: Jesus, who was once a child who grew taller and wiser, will help us make wise decisions as we grow.

I found these shoes hidden away in an old suitcase the other day. *Hold up pair of baby shoes.* Look how tiny they are. These shoes would only fit a small baby. While I was rummaging in that same suitcase, I also found these shoes. *Hold up child's shoes.* These shoes are much bigger than the baby shoes. They look like they would fit some of you.

Hold up both pairs of shoes. These shoes belonged to the same person. But that boy [girl] grew a whole lot from the time he [she] wore these baby shoes until he [she] fit into these much bigger shoes. Each of you was once small enough to fit into these baby shoes. But now look how big you are!

Jesus grew too. When He was born He was just a tiny baby. But soon He sat up, then He crawled, then He walked and even ran all by Himself. Jesus grew and grew and grew. Soon He was 12 years old, and He was able to go to Jerusalem with Mary and Joseph for the Feast of the Passover. While Jesus was in Jerusalem, He sat in the temple with the teachers and talked with them about God. Everyone who heard Jesus was amazed at His understanding and wise answers.

Jesus not only grew taller and bigger, He also grew in wisdom. Wisdom means obeying God and knowing what is right and what is wrong. Jesus knew He needed to learn about His Father in Heaven. When Mary and Joseph came looking for Him, Jesus asked them, "Didn't you know I had to be in My Father's house?" Then Jesus went back home to Nazareth because He also knew He needed to obey Mary and Joseph.

A person growing in wisdom is able to decide what is right and what is wrong. Do you think a wise person hits a friend when he is angry? *Let children reply to each question.* Do you think a wise person shares toys? Do you think a wise person cleans up her room?

We don't really do anything to grow taller and bigger. As long as we eat healthy foods, God makes our bodies grow. God will help us grow in wisdom too. If we ask Him, He will give us the wisdom to know what is right and what is wrong. He will guide us in making the best decisions for our lives.

God gives us something special to help us grow in wisdom. *Hold up Bible.* He gives us the Bible. *Open Bible.* It says, "The holy Scriptures ... are able to make you wise for salvation through faith in Christ Jesus" (2 Timothy 3:15). The Bible tells us all about Jesus and how He died to save us from our sins. Because of Jesus, God forgives us when we do wrong. God also gives us the strength to do what is right. God gives us true wisdom. Let's thank God for His goodness and help.

Prayer: Dear God, thank You for helping us grow. You make our bodies grow, and You also help us grow in wisdom so that we know what is right and what is wrong. Forgive us when we do wrong and give us the strength and wisdom to do what is right. Amen.

Like Son, Like Father

⟫⟩◈⟨⟪

SECOND SUNDAY AFTER CHRISTMAS:
John 1:1–18

Text: No one has ever seen God, but God the One and Only, who is at the Father's side, has made Him known. *John 1:18*

Teaching aids: Sheet of white paper, small paintbrush, cup of water, Bible, picture of Jesus.

Gospel truth: Jesus, who is true God, became man to suffer and die in our place so we could be saved from our sins. Because of Jesus, we know what God is like and we know how much He loves us.

Sit in front of the children with the sheet of white paper in your lap. Dip the paintbrush into the water and begin to "paint" as you talk. I love to paint. Sometimes my pictures are good, and sometimes they aren't so good. This picture is one of the good ones. Would you like to see it? *Hold up "painting."* Isn't it nice? Look! *Point to different spots on the "painting."* Here are the mountains. And here are the trees. And—this is the best part of all—here is the lake.

Do you like my painting? *Let the children respond.* I guess you're right. You can't see anything. But the mountains and trees and lake are there. I put them there just a few minutes ago.

Sometimes things are there that we can't see. You couldn't see my painting because the water was clear. We can't see the air we breathe, but it's all around us. We can't see the gravity that holds us onto earth, but it keeps us from floating into outer space. We can't see God, but He's with us all the time, everywhere we are.

We haven't seen God. but we see the beautiful world He made for us. We watch the snow fall, smell the flowers, touch the soft fur of a puppy, hear birds singing in the trees, and taste fresh summer strawberries. But we can't see, smell, touch, hear, or taste God.

God wanted us to know about Him even though we couldn't see Him. So He gave us the Bible to tell us who He is and what He has done for us. *Hold up Bible.* But God also loved us so much that He sent His only Son to earth. Do you know the name of God's Son? *Let children respond.* That's right. God called His Son Jesus because the name Jesus tells us that He is the Savior.

Hold up picture of Jesus. We can see Jesus. He was a real person just like we are. Jesus played and ate and laughed and cried. Jesus was just like us—except Jesus never sinned.

That's because Jesus is also true God. Jesus showed us what God is like. He showed us that God is powerful when He stopped raging storms with one word. He showed us that God is kind when He healed people who were sick. He showed us that God cares about us when He fed five thousand hungry people.

But most of all, Jesus showed us that God loves us because He was willing to suffer and die on the cross for our sins. Because of Jesus our sins are all forgiven. But Jesus didn't stay in the grave. On the third day, He came alive again. Only God could do that! And that means we will some-day live forever in heaven.

But right now God is with us all the time—at home or away, night or day, on earth or on the Milky Way. Jesus promised always to be with us, and He always keeps His promises. Let's thank Him!

Prayer: Thank You, dear God, for loving us so much. Thank You for sending Your Son, Jesus, to save us from our sins. Because of Jesus we know what You are like. And we love You too. Amen.

Remember Your Baptism

⟫◈⟪

THE BAPTISM OF OUR LORD:
Luke 3:15–17, 21–22

Text: When all the people were being baptized, Jesus was baptized too. And as He was praying, heaven was opened and the Holy Spirit descended on Him in bodily form like a dove. And a voice came from heaven: "You are My Son, whom I love; with You I am well pleased." *Luke 3:21–22*

Teaching aids: Baptismal font (optional), clear glass filled with water, Bible, large paper "drops of water" (one for each child) with these words written on each one: I am a child of God.

Gospel truth: When we are baptized, God forgives our sins, offers us eternal life, and makes us His own beloved children.

If possible, gather the children around the baptismal font. Have you ever been to church and seen someone— maybe a baby, maybe an older person—come here to the baptismal font to be baptized? *Let the children respond.* Baptism is a big word for a very important event. *Hold up a clear glass filled with water.* When a person is baptized, the pastor pours water on the person's head. Then the pastor says, "I baptize you in the name of the Father and of the Son and of the Holy Spirit." The words the pastor uses are important. *Hold up Bible.* These words were given to us by God in the Bible, and they are what makes Baptism so special.

John baptized many people while he was preaching in the desert. That's why they called him John the Baptist. One day Jesus came to the Jordan River to be baptized by John. After Jesus was baptized, a dove came down and rested on Him. Then a voice spoke from heaven. It said, "You are My Son, whom I love; with You I am well pleased." The dove was really the Holy Spirit, and the voice was God Himself speaking!

When we are baptized the Holy Spirit comes to us too. He comes into our hearts to create faith in Jesus. The Bible tells us that "whoever believes and is baptized will be saved" (Mark 16:16). The Holy Spirit causes our faith to grow and grow. He gives us strength to live as God wants us to live.

God gives us some special gifts when we are baptized. He washes away our sins and gives us the promise of life forever with Him in heaven. And we become part of God's family—one of His own children. What wonderful blessings those are!

Give each child a paper "drop of water." I'm going to give each of you a "drop of water" to remind you that Baptism with water and the Word of God makes you God's own child. It says: I am a child of God.

I have a poem that celebrates Baptism. Will you join me with the motions?

I was baptized, happy day!
> *Clap hands.*

All my sins were washed away.
> *Move hands back and forth as if erasing a blackboard.*

God looked down on me and smiled.
> *Point to self.*

I became His own dear child.
> *Hug self.*

(From *Little Ones Sing Praise,* copyright © 1989 Concordia Publishing House.)

Remember your own Baptism every day. Remember that

you are God's own child. He has forgiven your sins and given you the promise of eternal life.

Prayer: Dear God, help me to remember the blessings of my Baptism every day. Thank You for making me Your own child. Thank You for washing away my sins. Thank You for promising me eternal life. Amen.

A Real Friend

⟫⬥⟪

SECOND SUNDAY AFTER THE EPIPHANY: John 2:1–11

Text: Jesus said to the servants, "Fill the jars with water"; so they filled them to the brim. Then He told them, "Now draw some out and take it to the master of the banquet." They did so, and the master of the banquet tasted the water that had been turned into wine. ... This, the first of His miraculous signs, Jesus performed in Cana in Galilee. He thus revealed His glory, and His disciples put their faith in Him. *John 2:7–9, 11*

Teaching aids: Colorful birthday party invitation, several inflated balloons, multiplication flash card, Band-Aid.

Gospel truth: Jesus cares about our every need and is both willing and able to give us all we require. We can freely and confidently call on Him for help at all times.

Hold up birthday party invitation. This invitation arrived in the mail yesterday. I can't wait! One of my best friends is having a birthday party. It's going to be so much fun. *Hold up balloons.* We'll have balloons and presents and lots of cake and ice cream. I'm sure this will be a great party.

One time there was a party—actually it was a wedding feast—that went on for days and days. The bride and groom wanted their guests to have a good time. And they did! The guests ate lots of food, drank good wine, and talked to friends. But then the bride and groom ran out of wine. There was nothing for their guests to drink except water.

Jesus was at this wedding feast with His disciples and His mother, Mary. Mary knew the wedding feast wasn't nearly over and the bride and groom would be embarrassed and unhappy if their guests didn't have anything to drink. So she asked Jesus to help them. Jesus told the servants to fill six big jars with water. Then He told them to pour some of the water and take it to the man in charge of the feast. When the man drank it, he said, "That's the best wine I've ever tasted."

Jesus had turned the water into wine! It was the first miracle that He ever did. Jesus did many more miracles while He was preaching and teaching on earth. He healed blind and deaf and sick people. He walked on water and calmed fierce storms. He fed 5,000 people with five loaves of bread and two small fish.

But this miracle is special because it shows us that Jesus cares about all our problems. No matter how small or unimportant our problems might seem to other people, Jesus cares. And as true God He has the power to help us. Jesus didn't want the bride and groom to be embarrassed and unhappy because they didn't have enough wine for their wedding feast. So He helped them.

And Jesus helps us too. *Hold up flash card.* When you need help learning those multiplication tables, Jesus cares. *Hold up bandage.* When you fall off your bike and scrape your knee, Jesus cares. *Hold up birthday party invitation.* When you're not invited to the birthday party that all your other friends are going to, Jesus cares. Jesus always cares, and Jesus always loves you.

Jesus loves us so much that He gave His life for us. He's our Savior! But this story about how Jesus turned water into wine at a wedding feast reminds us that He's also our friend. He cares about everything in our lives, and He's always ready, willing, and able to help us. Now that's a real friend.

Prayer: Dear Jesus, You are my best friend. You care about everything that happens to me, no matter how small or unimportant it may seem to others. I know I can always come to You. Thank You, Jesus. Amen.

Set Free

THIRD SUNDAY AFTER THE EPIPHANY:
Luke 4:14–21

Text: "The Spirit of the Lord is on me, because He has anointed me to preach good news to the poor. He has sent me to proclaim freedom for the prisoners and recovery of sight for the blind, to release the oppressed, to proclaim the year of the Lord's favor." Then He rolled up the scroll, gave it back to the attendant and sat down. The eyes of everyone in the synagogue were fastened on Him, and He began by saying to them, "Today this scripture is fulfilled in your hearing." *Luke 4:18–21*

Teaching aids: Several feathers, small amount of oil in a container, a long sheet of paper rolled up like a scroll, large sheet of paper with these words written on it: Jesus is my Savior!

Gospel truth: Jesus, our Savior, has washed us clean and set us free from sin. This news makes us so happy we want to share it with everyone we meet.

Did you ever wonder how birds are able to stay warm when it's cold outside? *Hold up several feathers.* Their feathers keep them warm. They overlap them, fluff them up, and make their own layers of insulation.

But birds that live on beaches can get into trouble when there's an oil spill at sea. The oil pollutes the water, and the water washes onto the birds. Their feathers become coated with the sticky oil and flatten down. *Dip a feather into the oil.* The birds aren't able to fluff them up. So when cold water and weather come, the birds become chilled and die. The only way to save birds caught in an oil spill is to give them a soapy bath that washes the sticky oil off their feathers. Then the birds are free to take off and fly again.

In a way we are like birds caught in an oil spill. We are soaked with sin. Maybe we push other people around. Maybe we don't clean up our room when we are asked. Maybe we tell a lie because we think it will keep us out of trouble.

We are all soaked with sin, but Jesus washes our sin away and makes us clean. He suffered and died that we might have all our sins forgiven. Jesus is our Savior! He has washed away our sin! He has set us free!

The Bible tells us that one day Jesus went to the synagogue in Nazareth. He stood up to read from the scroll of the prophet Isaiah. The Bible in those days was written on scrolls like this. *Hold up "scroll."* These scrolls were kept in a special place in the temple. When someone wanted to read the scroll, he rolled up one side while he unrolled the other. *Roll and unroll scroll.*

Jesus unrolled the scroll and read several verses that promised the Savior would preach and heal and set His people free. Then Jesus rolled the scroll back up and sat down. He told all the people in the synagogue that He was not there to just read and teach God's Word. He was there to make those words come true. He was the Savior!

What exciting news that must have been so long ago. And it's still exciting news today! Jesus of Nazareth is the Savior! That news is so exciting and so happy that I want to share it with everyone I meet. Would you like to help me share that news?

Hold up large paper with message. This says: Jesus is my Savior. Let's all say those words together. *Hold up poster and say words together.* That wasn't very loud. I don't think too many people heard our good news. Let's try again, louder this time. *Repeat.* That was much better. But I'm still not sure the people way in the back row heard our good news. Let's try once more, really loud this time. *Repeat once more.* Wow! That was loud! I think everybody heard the good news this time. And good news like that needs to be shared with everyone!

Prayer: Dear Jesus, You are my Savior. You have washed my sin away and set me free. That news makes me so happy. Help me share that news with everyone I meet. Amen.

Never Alone

———◆———

FOURTH SUNDAY AFTER THE EPIPHANY:
Luke 4:21–32

Text: "I tell you the truth," He continued, "no prophet is accepted in his hometown." *Luke 4:24*

Teaching aid: A doll.

Gospel truth: Jesus, who was rejected by the people of Nazareth, understands our sorrows and promises to help us through them.

Hold up doll. This is Daisy. She's a hero. Last summer when she was swimming at the lake, she saved the life of a person who was drowning. But yesterday when Daisy told her friends at school about what happened at the lake, they didn't believe her. They all said she made up the whole story, and she didn't save anybody at all. Now Daisy's friends just ignore her and won't even talk to her.

How do you think Daisy feels now? *Let the children respond.* You're right, Daisy feels very sad. That's why I brought her with me today. I hoped you could cheer her up again because you know the true story. Daisy really is a hero.

Maybe you can remember a time you felt ignored and rejected like Daisy. Maybe you were the last person chosen for the baseball team. Or, maybe no one remembered your birthday. Or, maybe your best friend found a new best friend.

Jesus knows just how you felt. One time when He went to His hometown of Nazareth to teach in the synagogue, He told the people there that He was the promised Savior. The people of Nazareth had known Jesus since He was a little boy, and they were shocked at His words. When Jesus didn't perform a miracle to prove He was the Savior, the people became angry and tried to hurt Him.

Jesus was ignored and rejected by the people in His own hometown. How sad Jesus must have felt. But do you know what Jesus did? He walked right through the crowd of people trying to hurt Him and went on to the town of Capernaum. The people there listened to His teaching and believed.

Jesus knows how bad it feels when someone ignores us or rejects us because it happened to Him too. And He promises to always be there to help us through our sad times. We're never alone. Our best friend Jesus is always with us.

Jesus also knows that the sad times don't last forever. *Hold up doll.* Daisy's sad times ended when she came here and met all of you. Your sad times won't last long either. Maybe you'll be the captain of the baseball team or maybe you'll have the biggest birthday party ever or maybe you'll find a new best friend of your own.

The sad times are like rainy days. They help us to appreciate the sun when it shines again. But no matter what, rainy day or sunny day, your best friend Jesus is right by your side. He'll never leave you alone.

Prayer: Dear Jesus, it's so good to know that You understand our sorrows. You know what it's like to be ignored and rejected. But it's even better to know that You are always with us. No matter what, You are our best friend. Amen.

Follow the Leader

———⋙◈⋘———

FIFTH SUNDAY AFTER THE EPIPHANY:
Luke 5:1–11

Text: Then Jesus said to Simon, "Don't be afraid; from now on you will catch men." So they pulled their boats up on shore, left everything and followed Him. *Luke 5:10–11*

Teaching aid: None.

Gospel truth: Jesus calls us to follow Him and be His helpers. He will help us to do His work.

Today we're going to play a game called follow the leader. I will move different ways and I want each of you to follow me. Are you ready? *Lift your arm into the air. Turn your head from side to side. Wiggle your fingers. Clap your hands. Shake both your arms. Close your eyes. Smile.* That was good!

Follow the leader is a fun game to play. Today we're going to talk about some people in the Bible who "followed the leader." Who do you think their leader was? *Let the children respond.* That's right. Their leader was Jesus. When Jesus began to preach and teach, He chose people to follow Him. But they weren't playing a game. They had important work to do. Jesus wanted them to help Him do His work.

Jesus chose 12 people to be His helpers. *As you say the name of each disciple, raise another finger to "count" them.* Their names were Peter, Andrew, James, John, Philip, Bartholomew, Matthew, Thomas, James the son of Alphaeus, Simon, Thaddaeus, and Judas Iscariot.

Jesus found His helpers in different places doing different things. Before Jesus called him, Matthew was a tax collector in Capernaum while Peter, James, and John were all fishermen on the Lake of Galilee. Jesus' helpers also had very different personalities. Peter was enthusiastic and impulsive, Thomas tended to doubt things until they were proven to him, and James had a stormy temper.

Each of Jesus' helpers was an ordinary person. But through Jesus they became powerful workers for God. They went all over the land with Jesus. They listened and helped as He taught the people. They became Jesus' special friends.

Jesus still chooses helpers today. He chooses each of us to follow Him and do His work. No matter how old or how young you are, you can be a helper for Jesus. Each time you show love to someone else, that act shows love to Jesus. Each time you carry groceries or pick up toys or make a get well card for someone who is sick, you are Jesus' helper. Each time you set the table or comfort a friend who is hurt or bring a neighbor to Sunday school, you are Jesus' helper. How exciting to be a special helper and friend to Jesus!

Peter, James, John, and the rest of Jesus' 12 helpers didn't always know how to help Him. Sometimes they felt tired and grouchy and lazy. But Jesus always forgave them and gave them the courage and strength to go on. Jesus will give you the strength to be His helper too. On those days when the whole room seems filled with messy toys or the grocery bag feels so heavy or the whole sink is piled with dirty dishes, Jesus will help you. He will help you "follow the leader" and do His work. That's because Jesus loves you so much, and He chooses you to be His special friend.

Prayer: Dear Jesus, we want to follow You and be Your special helpers. But sometimes it's hard to follow You and do Your work. Sometimes we feel tired or just plain lazy. Give us strength to follow You. Be with us as we try to show Your love to people around us. Amen.

Blessed Are You

SIXTH SUNDAY AFTER THE EPIPHANY:
Luke 6:17–26

Text: Blessed are you who are poor, for yours in the kingdom of God. Blessed are you who hunger now, for you will be satisfied. Blessed are you who weep now, for you will laugh. *Luke 6:20–21*

Teaching aids: Paper bag filled with lots of foods including a banana, and a picture of Jesus.

Gospel truth: Jesus, who died for us and gave us the promise of eternal life, fills our hearts with His love. We rejoice in the salvation He offers and experience the joy that only God can give.

I am so-o-o hungry this morning. I didn't have time for breakfast, so I thought I'd bring my breakfast with me to church. *Hold up paper bag.* You don't mind, do you? *Reach into bag and pull out foods one by one. Then peel the banana and take a bite.*

My stomach feels much better now that I've had something to eat. *Begin putting foods back into paper bag.* I'll save these foods for later because I know I'll be hungry again in just a little while. That's the problem with food. It only lasts for a short time and then you get hungry again.

One time Jesus preached a sermon where He said, "Blessed are you who hunger now, for you will be satisfied." Most people wouldn't think that being hungry was something to be happy about. But Jesus wasn't just talking about the kind of hunger your stomach feels. He was talking about the kind of hunger your heart feels when it needs to be filled.

I only know one thing that can satisfy a hungry heart. *Hold up picture of Jesus.* Jesus fills our hungry hearts. He fills them and fills them until they are so full that they overflow with love for everyone we meet. And the best thing of all is that He keeps on filling our hearts so that they never need to be hungry again.

Jesus gives and gives and gives. He gives everything to those who have nothing. Jesus even gave His life for us. He died on the cross to save us from our sins. Now we have everything—we have eternal life!

In His sermon Jesus says that people who hunger for the kind of food only He can give them are blessed. *Blessed* means a lot more than just happy. We are happy only until something comes along and makes us sad. But *blessed* means that we have the kind of joy that only God can give. Deep down joy that lasts forever because we know that Jesus is our Savior and we belong to Him.

The word *blessed* reminds me of the song that says:

I have the joy, joy, joy, joy down in my heart,
Down in my heart, down in my heart!
I have the joy, joy, joy, joy down in my heart,
Down in my heart to stay!

Will you join me in some actions to this song? *Repeat song above but add the following actions: Clap when you say the word "joy" and point to your heart when you say the word "heart."*

Prayer: Dear Jesus, thank You for giving everything to those who have nothing. Thank You for filling our hearts with Your love and giving us the kind of joy that only You can give. Amen.

Listen to Him

—⟫◈⟪—

THE TRANSFIGURATION OF OUR LORD: Luke 9:28–36

Text: A voice came from the cloud, saying, "This is My Son, whom I have chosen; listen to Him." *Luke 9:35*

Teaching aids: A Bible and a pillowcase or bag containing the following items: two pieces of sandpaper to rub together, a bell, a jar filled with beans, two spoons to hit together, and some coins to jingle.

Gospel truth: God sent His own Son, Jesus, to be our Savior from sin and death. We can hear this message of redemption in God's own word, the Bible.

I want you all to listen carefully. See if you can identify each of the sounds I'm going to make. *Reach into bag and use items inside to make different sounds. Let the children try to identify each sound as you make it. Show them each item after they have guessed.* Those were good guesses. You have to listen carefully to hear all those sounds, don't you?

Listening is an important skill we all need. Sometimes it's hard to listen. Instead we want to talk all the time. Or, we want to wiggle and play. Or, maybe we just want to make a lot of noise.

One time Jesus took three of His helpers—Peter, James, and John—to the top of a high mountain to pray. All at once Jesus' face shone like the sun and His clothing lit up like lightning! Then Moses and Elijah appeared next to Jesus and talked to Him. Peter, James, and John had been very sleepy, but when they saw what was happening, they woke right up. Peter wanted to make this special moment last longer, so he said, "Master, let's put up three shelters—one for You, one for Moses, and one for Elijah."

While Peter was talking, a cloud appeared and wrapped around them. A voice came from the cloud, saying, "This is My Son, whom I have chosen." It was God Himself speaking to them! Then the voice said one more thing to Peter, James, and John. "Listen to Him!" God said.

Listen to Him! God told these three helpers of Jesus to listen to Him. Listening to Jesus must be very important if God Himself told Peter, James, and John to do it. Listening to Jesus is important for us too. We have Jesus' words right here in the Bible. *Hold up Bible.*

Sometimes we pretend to listen to Jesus' words, but we really don't hear them. Our minds are thinking about the baseball game we're going to in a few hours or our fingers are drawing little pictures along the sides of our Sunday school paper or our feet are busy kicking the person sitting across from us. That's not real listening.

Real listening means that we hear Jesus' words not only with our ears but also with our hearts. We learn what Jesus' words mean for us and remember them.

And what wonderful words they are! Jesus tells us how much He loves us. He tells us that He died for our sins and rose again after three days. He tells us that someday we will live with Him in heaven forever. *Hold up Bible as you read the poem below.*

> Listen! Listen! And you will hear,
> The words of Jesus ring loud and clear.
> Jesus loves you. Jesus loves me.
> From sin and death He has set us free!

Prayer: Dear Jesus, thank You for loving us so much and dying on the cross to save us from our sins. Help us to show You how much we love You. Help us to really listen to Your words, not just with our ears but with our hearts too. Amen.

The Winning Team

FIRST SUNDAY IN LENT:
Luke 4:1–13

Text: Jesus answered, "It is written: 'Worship the Lord your God and serve Him only.' " *Luke 4:8*

Teaching aids: A cap, jersey, or jacket that is part of a team sport uniform; a Bible.

Gospel truth: The devil would like nothing better than to tempt believers away from God and His saving grace through Jesus. If we keep our eyes focused on Jesus and follow His example, He will help us overcome temptation, serve God, and win the ultimate victory.

Hold up the uniform. Do you know what this is? When would you wear it? *Let children respond.* When someone wears this uniform, you know that he or she is part of a team. A team has a captain, a coach, and a rule book. The captain is in charge of the whole team. The coach helps the team players learn the important plays. And the rule book helps everyone understand how to play the game. When everything comes together just right, the team wins the victory.

We are all part of a winning team. God the Father is our captain. Jesus is our coach, and the Bible is our rule book. We don't even need a uniform. When we do things God's way, follow Jesus, and obey His commands in the Bible, people will know that we are on God's winning team. They will see the things that we do and listen to the words that we say and they will know Jesus is the coach of our team.

But there is a problem. Every team has an opponent that it plays against. The opponent works hard to make the team lose the game. Our team, God's team, has an opponent too. Do you know who we are fighting against? *Let the children respond.* We are fighting against the devil, and he is the meanest, nastiest, strongest opponent of all! Not only does the devil want us to lose the most important battle of our lives, but he wants us to leave God's team and join his team.

The devil even wanted Jesus to join his team. In today's Gospel lesson we learn that Jesus went out to the desert by Himself. When Jesus was out there, He didn't eat any food. He got tired, hungry, and weak. The devil came out to the desert and tried to tempt Jesus. He wanted Jesus to turn away from God the Father and to worship him instead.

But Jesus knew how to fight His opponent. Jesus told the devil the words that were written in the Bible. He said, "It is written: 'Worship the Lord, your God, and serve Him only.' " When the devil figured out that he could not win against Jesus, he left Jesus alone in the desert.

Hold up the Bible. You and I can learn how to resist the devil's temptations also. The Bible tells us how. When we know and trust that Jesus has won the battle for us, we will be on the winning team. The devil will know that Jesus is on our team and that Jesus has already defeated him once and for all. Jesus already won the most important battle against the devil. He died on the cross for us and rose again so that all believers can live with Him in heaven someday.

The devil does not want us to go to heaven, and he will try very hard to make us turn away from God's winning team to join his team instead. He wants us to stop learning about the Bible and to stop believing in Jesus. But we know that God is the captain of our team and we know that Jesus is our coach. Every day we can trust Jesus to defeat the devil for us and we can learn from God's Word, the Bible. What a winning combination!

Prayer: Dear God, thank You for sending Your Son, Jesus, to be our Savior. Help us learn to follow His example so that the devil will turn away from us too. Help us remember each day that we are part of Your winning team. Amen.

Staying on Track and Reaching the Goal

SECOND SUNDAY IN LENT:
Luke 13:31–35

Text: "… on the third day I will reach my goal." *Luke 13:32b*

Teaching aids: An Energizer battery, two first-place ribbons (paper or cloth), a safety pin.

Gospel truth: Because of the death and resurrection of Jesus, those who believe in Him will someday reach their goal in heaven.

Let's play a guessing game. I'll say something to describe someone and you tell me who I am describing. Here's the first one. "He keeps going and going and going …" Who am I talking about? *Hold up Energizer battery.* I'm talking about the Energizer bunny. The commercial tells us that when he uses the Energizer battery, nothing can stop him.

Now, who do you think I am describing? "And he wins by a nose …" *Hold up the blue ribbons.* I'm talking about the winner of a race. Sometimes when a race is really close, they say that the winner wins by a nose. When the winner is running toward the goal, nothing can stop him.

Now, I am going to describe someone else, but I will not use any words. Watch what I do. *Form a cross with the blue ribbons. Use the safety pin to hold the ribbons together. Show the cross to the children.* Who do you think I am describing? Yes, it's Jesus. There was nothing that could stop Jesus from reaching His goal.

What do you think was the goal that Jesus was trying to reach? What did He come to earth to do for us? *Hold up the ribbon cross again.* Jesus came to live a perfect life here on earth so He could die for us and rise again. His goal was to make it possible for every believer to live with Him eternally in heaven. Every day that Jesus lived on earth He was one step closer to the goal, and nothing was going to stop Him. That's how important this goal was to Jesus.

Every day we get closer and closer to a very important goal. Our goal is to live forever with Him in heaven. An Energizer battery will not help us reach the goal of heaven, even a blue ribbon cannot help us. Instead, we have the power of the Holy Spirit to help us keep believing so we can reach our goal.

It will not be easy trying to reach this goal. When a runner is running a race, she needs to keep her eyes on the finish line. That is the goal she is trying to reach. It helps her to focus and to know where she is going so she can keep on track. We need to keep our eyes focused on Jesus so we can stay on track.

Sometimes other things might try to get in the way and take our eyes away from Jesus and the goal of heaven. Let's say you like sports. Well, someone might try to tell you that practicing with the team is more important than going to church. But that would take your eyes off of Jesus and the goal of heaven. Someone might even try to tell you that stealing or telling a lie or hurting someone is more important than obeying God's commandments. But that would take your eyes off Jesus and the goal of heaven.

Hold up the ribbon cross. Always remember that Jesus did not let anything stop Him from reaching His goal of being our Savior. Keep your eyes focused on the cross of Jesus and you will stay on track too!

Prayer: Dear Jesus, we know that You stayed on track and reached Your goal of being our Savior. Nothing could stop You from giving Your life on the cross for our sins. We thank You for being our Savior, and we ask You to help us stay on track too. Help us keep our eyes focused on You so we will someday reach our goal and live in heaven with You. Amen.

R-E-P-E-N-T

THIRD SUNDAY IN LENT:
Luke 13:1–9

Text: But unless you repent, you too will all perish. *Luke 13:3*

Teaching aids: White poster board, six index cards, masking tape. Cut the poster board into one 5″ × 20″ sheet and one 5″ × 35″ sheet. Place the short piece horizontally over the long piece. Fasten the pieces together with a paper fastener. Print one of the following letters on each index card—R-E-P-E-N-T.

Gospel truth: Salvation is ours through Jesus' death and resurrection, yet we are called to repent.

Select two volunteers to come forward and hold the poster board horizontally between them. Tape the index card with the "R" to the left of the horizontal short piece. Let me tell you a story about Robert. One day Robert was visiting his grandparents. He was playing catch with a football. Robert wanted to show off for his friend, so he threw the ball extra hard. The ball broke one of the windows. He realized what he had done was wrong. He asked for forgiveness, and he played catch in another place.

Add the card marked "E." Let me tell you a story about Elizabeth. One day Elizabeth was waiting for the school bus. Some girls started to talk about a new little girl. They started to make fun of her, and Elizabeth joined in. When she turned around, Elizabeth saw that the little girl was listening. Elizabeth realized that what she had done was wrong. She asked for forgiveness and invited the little girl to sit on the bus with her.

Add the card marked "P." Let me tell you a story about Pedro. One day Pedro was taking a math test. It was a hard test. When he didn't know the answers, Pedro copied the answers from his neighbor's paper. The teacher caught him cheating. He realized what he had done was wrong, and Pedro asked for forgiveness. He took the test over and did the very best he could without cheating.

Add the card marked "E." Let me tell you a story about Erin. One day Erin was playing in the sandbox. Her friend took away the shovel that she wanted to use. Erin got angry and pushed the little girl down. Sand got into her eyes and the little girl started to cry. Erin realized that what she had done was wrong and she asked for forgiveness. She let her friend use the shovel, and she used another scoop instead.

Add the card marked "N." Let me tell you a story about Nick. One day Nick was changing clothes in his bedroom. His mom told him to pick up all of his dirty clothes. Nick said no and ran outside. After a while, Nick realized that what he had done was wrong, and he asked for forgiveness. He picked up all his clothes and put them in the laundry basket.

Add the card marked "T." Let me tell you a story about Theresa. One day Theresa was playing at a friend's house. She saw that her friend had a new ring that she really wanted. When her friend wasn't looking, she took the ring and put it in her pocket. After she got home, Theresa realized that what she had done was wrong. She went back to her friend's house and asked for forgiveness. She gave back the ring.

All these children have some things in common. Can you tell me what it is? *Let the children respond.* They all did something wrong. That's called sin. They all realized that their sin was wrong and asked for forgiveness. Then they stopped doing the sin. *Point to the word "repent."* There is a word that describes all these things put together. That word is "repent."

In today's Gospel lesson, Jesus tells people that they must repent. *Twist the longer piece of poster board down into a vertical position to make a cross.* Jesus took all our sins to the cross when He died and rose again. We know that our sins are forgiven, but it is important to use the power of the Holy Spirit to realize the wrong things we do, ask forgiveness, and to stop doing them. We can rejoice in the gift of forgiveness and someday we all will rejoice in heaven.

Prayer: Dear Jesus, we know that we sin and do things we know are wrong. Help us to repent and do those things that are good instead. Thank You for the gift of forgiveness and the gift of salvation. Amen.

Repent! Rejoice!

———>·◆·<———

FOURTH SUNDAY IN LENT:
Luke 15:1–3, 11–32

Text: Let's have a feast and celebrate. For this son of mine ... was lost and is found. *Luke 15:23–24*

Teaching aids: Red and white crepe paper. Cut enough 1′ red streamers and 1′ white streamers so each child has one streamer. Cut one 2′ red streamer and one 2′ white streamer and one 3′ red and one 3′ white streamer.

Gospel truth: Through His grace, Jesus gives repentant sinners the gift of salvation. There is rejoicing in heaven each time a sinner repents.

Hold up a 2′ red streamer and a 2′ white streamer. Wow! It looks as if we could have a party! We have crepe paper for decorations, and now all we need is a reason to celebrate. What do you think we could celebrate? *Let children respond.* Those are all good reasons to celebrate. A celebration is a time of rejoicing. When we celebrate, we show how happy we feel.

In today's Gospel lesson we hear the story of a father who calls for a celebration. His son left home and did some foolish things for which he was sorry. When the son came back to repent and ask for his father's forgiveness, the father said, "Let's have a feast and celebrate. For this son of mine was ... lost and is found!" The father's heart was full of forgiveness and happiness. He loved his son and rejoiced because his son had seen the wrong things he had done and had come back to the father for forgiveness. The son repented and the father rejoiced.

Our heavenly Father is like the father in the story. He rejoices with the angels in heaven each time one of His children on earth repents. *Hold the red streamer in one hand and the white streamer in the other hand. Wave the red streamer each time you say* **repent.** *Wave the white streamer each time you say* **rejoice.** Repent! *Wave the red streamer.* Rejoice! *Wave the white streamer.* Repent! *Wave the red streamer.* Rejoice! *Wave the white streamer.*

Hand out 1' streamers to each child. Alternate between red and white. I would like you to help me with this celebration cheer. When we say, "Repent!" those of you with red streamers stand up and wave your streamers. Then sit down. When we say, "Rejoice!" those of you with white streamers stand up and wave your streamers. Then sit down. Let's practice. Repent! *Red.* Rejoice! *White.* Repent! *Red.* Rejoice! *White.*

You and I are like the son in the story. We sin each and every day. What are some of the sins we do? *Let the children respond.* We repent when we know that we have sinned, ask for forgiveness, and use the power of the Holy Spirit to stop doing the sin. And when we repent, our Father in heaven rejoices. Repent! *Red.* Rejoice! *White.* Repent! *Red.* Rejoice! *White.*

Select a child to hold one end of the 3' white and one end of the 3' red streamer together. Begin to twist the pieces together as you talk. Our Father in heaven rejoices when we repent because He sent Jesus to die for our sins. The red streamer reminds me of the blood Jesus shed on the cross for us. Our Father in heaven rejoices when we repent because He sent Jesus to die for our sins and rise again on Easter so all believers could rejoice eternally in heaven. The white streamer reminds me of the glory we will see in heaven someday. *Select a child to hold the ends of the twisted streamer. Have the children hold the streamers horizontally at chest level. Select two other children and twist together the 2' red and white streamers. Have these children hold their piece across the longer streamer to form a cross.*

There are many more people that need to hear the news that Jesus took our sins to the cross. There are many more people that need to realize their sins and repent. We can tell others the good news of salvation so they can repent and there can be rejoicing in heaven. Repent! *Red.* Rejoice! *White.* Repent! *Red.* Rejoice! *White.*

Prayer: Dear God, our heavenly Father, fill us with the Holy Spirit so we might repent of our sins. Help us to know that You rejoice each time a sinner repents. Help us share the good news of heavenly rejoicing with others. Amen.

Choosing the Right Thing

———◆———

FIFTH SUNDAY IN LENT:
Luke 20:9–19

Text: The stone the builders rejected has become the cap-stone. *Luke 20:17b*

Teaching aids: A flashlight with working batteries; other items that could fit into the flashlight instead of batteries such as a small comb, a crayon, and a pencil eraser.

Gospel truth: Though others might reject Him, Jesus is the capstone, and it is only through Him that salvation can be won.

Show the flashlight to the children and turn it on and off. I brought a flashlight with me today. I know that every time I turn the switch, my flashlight will go on. Do you know why? It's because my flashlight has batteries. If I take out the batteries, what will happen? *Take out the batteries and turn on the flashlight.* You are right! The flashlight will not work without the batteries.

But I brought some other things that fit into that spot for the batteries. Maybe they will work. Let's give them a try. *Show the comb and place it in the flashlight.* This comb fits just right! Let's see if it works. *Turn on the flashlight.* No, the comb is the wrong thing for making this flashlight work. Let's try a marking pen. *Remove the comb and put in a marking pen. Turn on the flashlight.* No, the marking pen is the wrong thing for making this flashlight work. Let's try a pencil eraser. *Take out the marking pen and put in the eras-*

er. Turn on the flashlight. No, this eraser is the wrong thing for making the flashlight work.

Remove the eraser and hold up the comb, marking pen, and eraser. The comb did not work, the marking pen did not work, and the eraser did not work. I would be making the wrong decision if I chose one of these, wouldn't I? What is the only thing that will make this flashlight work? *Let the children respond.* That's right! The right thing to choose would be the batteries. *Put the batteries in again and turn on the flashlight.* If you had to choose between the batteries, comb, marking pen, and eraser, what would you choose to make the flashlight work? *Let the children respond.*

Today's Gospel lesson talks about people who choose the wrong thing instead of the right thing. For many years, God's people had been told that He would send them a Savior. When God sent Jesus to be the Savior of His people, some people did not believe that He was God's Son. They rejected Him. Even after Jesus died on the cross and rose again, some people chose not to believe that Jesus was the way to heaven. They did not choose the right thing.

The flashlight will not work without batteries. Salvation will not work without Jesus. It is important to remember this because some people might tell you there are other ways to get to heaven. They might tell you that if you do enough good things for others, you will get to heaven. But that would be choosing "doing good things" instead of choosing Jesus. Or, they might tell you that being an important person is the way to get to heaven. But that would be choosing "being important" instead of choosing Jesus.

We know we will go to heaven someday because the Holy Spirit has helped us to choose Jesus. Remember how foolish it was to put a comb or a marking pen or an eraser in the flashlight? It is even more foolish to choose any other way to get to heaven. Jesus is the only way to heaven. Choosing Jesus is choosing the right thing.

Prayer: Dear Jesus, fill us with the power of the Holy Spirit so we might always remember that You are the only way to heaven. Amen.

The Right Fit

═══◆═══

PALM SUNDAY:
Luke 22:1–23:56

Texts: The centurion, seeing what had happened, praised God and said, "Surely this was a righteous man." *Luke 23:47*

"Surely this man was the Son of God." *Mark 15:39b*

Teaching aids: A glove, a card that fits inside the glove, masking tape. On one side of the card, draw a cross. On the other side of the card, write the word sin. Roll a piece of masking tape and stick it just inside the glove. (Optional: a washable marking pen.)

Gospel truth: All people are sinners. God provided a Savior through His Son, Jesus Christ. Through His death on the cross and resurrection, Jesus won redemption for all.

Place the card in the glove and put the glove on your hand. As you talk, turn your hand back and forth so that everyone can see how the glove fits. This glove fits my hand just right. Sometimes my hand gets cold, but the glove will keep it warm. Sometimes my hand gets dirty, but the glove will keep it clean. Sometimes my hand gets scratched, but the glove will protect it. The glove is just the right fit no matter what my hand needs.

Remove the card. Show the children the side of the card that says "sin." All people are sinners. We all have done things that are wrong. Some have told lies, others have hurt people, and still others have taken things that don't belong to them. Can you name other sins that people do? *Let the children respond.*

We all sin and we all need to be saved from our sins, no

matter what those sins are. Just like this glove fits my hand just right, God has something that fits all sinners just right and can save them from their sins. *Remove the masking tape and place it in on the palm of the glove. Turn the card over so the children see the cross and stick the card on the tape.* God sent Jesus to take our sins to the cross with Him. When He died on the cross, He took the punishment for our sins. Jesus could do this for us because He was the Son of God sent to be our Savior.

When Jesus died on the cross, lots of people were watching. One of those people was called a centurion. He was a soldier standing guard. When the centurion saw what happened when Jesus died, he realized that Jesus was the Son of God. Jesus died for the centurion's sins just like He died for your sins and mine.

Raise your hands above your head in a posture of praise. On the first Palm Sunday, people raised palms in their hands as a way to show their praise to Jesus. Today, on this Palm Sunday, we can raise our hands in praise. Can you raise your hands in praise?

Reach out to the children with your gloved hand, palm side up. Today, on this Palm Sunday, we also can reach out to others with the cross of Jesus. We can share the love of Jesus by doing kind things. We can ask for forgiveness and forgive those who have sinned against us. And we can tell others about what Jesus has done for us. We can shake the hand of a friend close by and say, "Jesus loves you. Jesus died for you." Jesus is the right fit for all sinners and everyone needs to hear this good news. Jesus is the right fit for you and for me.

Prayer: Dear God, our Father in heaven, thank You for sending Your Son, Jesus Christ, to be our Savior. We are all sinners and we know that Jesus died for us. Help us share the news of Jesus' love with others. Amen.

His Name Is Jesus

━━▷◦◁━━

THE RESURRECTION OF OUR LORD:
Luke 24:1–11

Text: He is not here; He has risen! *Luke 24:6a*

Teaching aids: A bag and a picture of Jesus. Place the picture in the bag.

Gospel truth: When Jesus rose on Easter, the darkness of death was cast away and the light of victory shone all around. Jesus lives for us today and throughout all eternity.

Close your eyes as tightly as you can. What do you see? It is very dark and dismal. It seems very black, very empty, and very sad. Open your eyes. When Jesus died on the cross, His friends thought they would never see Him again. They felt dark, dismal, and empty inside.

Close your eyes again. *Take the picture of Jesus out of the bag and hold it up for all to see.* Open your eyes! What do you see now? *Let the children respond.* Yes, you see a picture of Jesus. The darkness is gone and in the light you see Jesus. On the first Easter, the darkness and sadness of Jesus' friends was gone when they discovered that He had risen!

Continue to hold up the picture of Jesus. If I were to keep on holding this picture and you were to close your eyes, would Jesus still be here for you? Yes, He would! Jesus is here for you every day and every night. He died once and rose again a long time ago, and He continues to live for you. Some day, you will see Jesus face to face in heaven where we will live with Him forever.

I am going to lead you in a song. I will do a part and you will do a part. The signal for your turn will be this: *Raise your hands above your head.* Every time I raise my hands above my head, you raise your hands and shout, "His name is Jesus!" Let's practice. *Raise your hands and lead the children in their part.*

Sing the following stanzas to the melody, "Mary Had a Little Lamb." You can chant the text if you don't sing.

Do you know who died for you,
    Died for you, died for you?
Do you know who died for you? *Raise your hands.*
    His name is Jesus!

Do you know who rose for you,
    Rose for you, rose for you?
Do you know who rose for you? *Raise your hands.*
    His name is Jesus!

Do you know who lives for you,
    Lives for you, lives for you?
Do you know who lives for you? *Raise your hands.*
    His name is Jesus!

Remember each and every day the good news that we celebrate this Easter. Jesus died for you. He rose for you. He lives for you! Who is our Savior? *Raise your hands.* His name is Jesus!

Prayer: Dear Jesus, what a happy day today is! We celebrate your resurrection. You are alive for us today and every day. Help us to remember Your resurrection every day and fill us with Your love. Amen.

Believing without Seeing

<hr>

SECOND SUNDAY OF EASTER:
John 20:19–31

Text: Blessed are those who have not seen and yet have believed. *John 20:29b*

Teaching aids: A shoe box with a $10 bill taped under the lid; a Bible.

Gospel truth: Through the power of the Holy Spirit, we can believe in Jesus even though we cannot see Him. The Holy Spirit works faith in our hearts through the sacraments and God's Word, the Bible.

Hold up the box for the children to see. What if I told you there was a $10 bill inside this box. Would you believe me? *Shake the box.* You can't see the money, and you can't hear it when I shake the box. How can you make sure there is really some money inside the box? *Let the children respond.* If you see the money, will you believe me? You know what they say, "Seeing is believing!"

Remove the lid and place it against your chest with the money side towards you. Show the children the empty box. Look! The box is empty! There is no money here. Do you still believe me?

This reminds me of the disciple named Thomas. After Jesus became alive again on Easter, He came to see the disciples gathered in a room. They could touch Him and talk to Him. They saw Him and they believed He was alive. But Thomas was not there. When Thomas came back and his friends told him about Jesus, Thomas did not believe Jesus was alive. All he knew was that the tomb was empty. He said he wouldn't believe that Jesus was alive until he saw Him. Jesus came back to the room the very next week and this time Thomas could see Jesus and he could touch Jesus. Now he believed that Jesus was alive. For Thomas, seeing was believing.

We can't see Jesus, but we believe in Him. We can't see Jesus, but we know that He is alive. We believe even though we can't see. This is called faith. God the Holy Spirit works faith in our hearts and helps us believe even though we cannot see.

Show the Bible. What book is this? *Let the children respond.* Yes, that's right. It is God's Word, the Bible. Every word in the Bible is true. When we read the Bible and learn about Jesus, we know that what we learn is true. The Bible tells us that Jesus died for our sins and rose again on Easter. The Bible tells us that Jesus is alive and that we will live forever with Him in heaven. We cannot see Jesus, but we believe!

Do you remember the $10 bill that I told you was in the box? You couldn't see it, so you didn't believe me! *Turn the lid over and show the money to the children.* But look! Even though you couldn't see it, the money was there all the time. You couldn't see it, but you could believe it! Even though we cannot see Jesus, He is alive and with us all the time. We cannot see Him, but we can believe in Him. Faith is believing without seeing.

Prayer: Thank You, God, for sending the Holy Spirit to help us believe even without seeing! Help us learn more and more about Jesus as we hear the good news shared with us in the Bible. Help us to share this good news with others. Amen.

Decoding the Message

THIRD SUNDAY OF EASTER: John 21:1–14

Text: Then the disciple whom Jesus loved said to Peter, "It is the Lord!" *John 21:7a*

Teaching aids: A chart showing the following coded message and a chart showing the key for the code; a piece of blank chart paper; a marking pen.

Message: (Draw each shape or mark in the order listed) cross, circle, star, rectangle, star, (leave a space), check, star, (leave a space), heart, square, check, wavy line, circle.

Code: Make the chart for the key to read as follows: cross = J, circle = E, star = S, rectangle = U, check = I, heart = A, square = L, wavy line = V.

Gospel truth: Jesus appeared to the disciples so that they might be reassured through the power of His resurrection. When we focus upon the risen Christ, we have the assurance of salvation.

Show the coded message. Can you read my message? You see my message, but you cannot understand it. Are you confused? *Show the chart with the key to the code.* This will help you understand. *Work out the code with the children. Use the marking pen to write the message on the blank chart paper.* There, now you can understand. The message reads, "Jesus is alive!" That is the message of Easter, and it fills our hearts with joy.

Sometimes, however, we can't understand the message so well. We let other things confuse us. We let other things become more important than the message of Jesus.

For example, what if you were chosen to play on your favorite softball team? You would be so happy and anxious to try your best. But what if you had to practice on Sunday morning? What if the coach told you that if you did not come to Sunday morning practice, you would be kicked off the team? If you went to softball practice, you would have to miss church and Sunday school. If you went to church and Sunday school, you would be kicked off the team.

That's a hard decision to make. You would probably feel confused. But if you let softball practice become more important than church and Sunday school, you might forget about the message of Jesus.

Or, what if a new boy and girl moved in next door and you really wanted to be their best friend. As you spent time with your new friends, you discovered that they did things that were wrong. They talked back to their parents. They made fun of other children. They even stole some candy from the store. Then they told you that if you wanted to be their friend, you would have to do the same kinds of things, even though you knew they were wrong.

That's a hard decision to make. You would probably feel confused. But if you let friends become more important than doing what is right, you might forget about the message of Jesus.

One day after Jesus rose on Easter, He was standing on the shore while His friends were fishing in a boat. They had tried all night to catch fish, but they had caught nothing. When they looked at the man on the shore, they didn't know it was Jesus. They were confused. Then the man told them where to put their nets, and they caught a whole net full of fish. After they saw this miracle, they understood. The disciple named John said, "It is the Lord!" They quickly went ashore to join their friend and Savior.

When we put Jesus first, before softball practice and friends, we will remember the message of Jesus' love. *Hold up the coded message.* We will remember that Jesus is alive and that someday we will join Him in heaven. That's the most important message of all. It is more important than softball practice and doing wrong things just to please our friends. Putting Jesus first will help us remember the message of salvation so that we can decode all the confusing messages.

Prayer: Dear Jesus, help us keep the message of Your love first in our lives. When we feel confused, help us think about You and remember what You would have us do. Help us share the message of Your love with others. Amen.

Snatch and Catch

───◆───

FOURTH SUNDAY OF EASTER:
John 10:22–30

Text: My sheep listen to My voice; I know them, and they follow Me. I give them eternal life, and they shall never perish; no one can snatch them out of My hand. *John 10:27–28*

Teaching aids: A cane, a drawing of a cane, or a pipe cleaner twisted into the shape of cane with a crook at the end.

Gospel truth: The people of God, those who believe in the death and resurrection of Jesus, will have eternal life.

Show the cane to the children. Can you tell me what this is? *Let the children respond.* Yes, it's a cane. People usually use a cane to help them walk. Today, however, let's imagine that this is a shepherd's staff that belonged to a shepherd who lived a long time ago.

Hold the cane out over the heads of the children, reaching out as if to snatch something as you discuss each example. The shepherd would use the staff to protect his sheep. If a wolf or a bear came close to his sheep, the shepherd would chase the intruder away and bring the sheep back to him for protection.

If one of the sheep wandered away and headed for a cliff, the shepherd would reach out and catch the sheep and bring it back to him before it went over the edge of the cliff. Whenever there was danger, the shepherd would use his staff for protection. Nothing could snatch one of the sheep away from the protecting shepherd. In fact, the shepherd loved his sheep so much that, if necessary, he would die to save his sheep.

In today's Gospel lesson, Jesus calls Himself a shepherd. We are the sheep He loves and protects. He loved us so much that He died for us so we could live forever in heaven. He gave us eternal life, and now He watches over us to protect us.

Again, hold the cane over the heads of the children and reach out as if to snatch something as you discuss each example. Jesus loves us just like the shepherd loved his sheep. He tells us that nothing can snatch us away from Him. If sin tries to snatch us away, Jesus will reach out and bring us back to Him where He forgives us and helps us do those things that are right. If fear tries to snatch us away, Jesus will reach out and bring us back to Him and reassure us that He is with us always. If we start to forget about our shepherd and wander away, He will reach out and catch us and bring us back to Him. In fact, Jesus loves us so much that if something tries to snatch us, Jesus always will reach out and catch us.

Prayer: Thank You, Jesus, for being our shepherd. Thank You for loving us and protecting us. Most of all, thank You for dying for us so that You could give us eternal life. Amen.

Love One Another

———✦◆✦———

FIFTH SUNDAY OF EASTER:
John 13:31–35

Text: A new command I give you: Love one another. As I have loved you, so you must love one another. By this all men will know that you are My disciples, if you love one another. *John 13:34–35*

Teaching aids: An apron, a hammer, chalk, an eraser, and one hug coupon for each child. The hug coupons can be index cards.

Gospel truth: When it comes to following the command to love one another, our standard is Christ's love for us. It is the mark of Christ's followers.

Hold up the apron. When you see someone wearing an apron, you can guess what he or she is doing. If I put on this apron, what do you think I would be getting ready to do? *Let the children respond.* Yes, that's right! I would be getting ready to cook. An apron is the mark of a cook.

Hold up the hammer. When you see someone holding a hammer, you can guess what he or she is doing. What do you think I would be getting ready to do with this hammer? *Let the children respond.* Yes, that's right. I would be getting ready to build or to fix something. A hammer is the mark of a carpenter.

Hold up the chalk and eraser. When you see someone holding chalk and an eraser, you can guess what he or she is doing. What do you think I could do with this chalk and eraser? *Let the children respond.* Yes, that's right. I would be getting ready to write something down for you to learn. Chalk and an eraser are the mark of a teacher.

You can figure lots of things out about a person just by watching him or her. You can tell which baseball team people like by looking at the kind of baseball caps they wear. You can tell when someone is in a hurry just by watching him run. You can tell when someone is loving and kind just by watching the things she does and listening to the things she says.

What are some things that kind and loving people do for others? *Let the children respond.* Those were all good ideas. Kind and loving people put other people first and love them in the same way that Jesus loves them.

In our Gospel lesson today, Jesus tells us to love one another as He has loved us. Just think about how much Jesus loves you and me. He loves us so much that He died for us on the cross. He knew it would hurt a lot, but He knew it was very important for us. He decided to do what was good for us instead of thinking about how much it would hurt.

There are lots of times that we can show love to our family and friends. Sometimes it might mean giving them something that we would rather keep for ourselves. Or, it might mean missing our favorite TV show because our friend wants to tell us about a bad day. Or, maybe it means sharing half of your very favorite candy bar because you want to share. When people see us doing those things, they know that we love Jesus and we are sharing His love with others. Sharing His love is the mark of a follower of Jesus.

Show a hug coupon. I brought something along today for each one of you to take home. It's called a hug coupon. You can give it to your mom or your dad or someone else you love. They will give it back to you when they need a hug. Then you can give the coupon to someone else so they can get a hug from you. When you give one of your very best bear hugs, remember to say, "Jesus loves you and so do I!" *Hand the coupons out to each child as they leave.*

Prayer: Dear Jesus, help us learn to love others the way You have loved us. Help us to be kind, loving, and unselfish. Help others to see Your love in things that we do and say. Amen.

The Gift That Lasts Forever

SIXTH SUNDAY OF EASTER:
John 14:23–29

Text: Peace I leave with you; My peace I give you. *John 14:27a*

Teaching aids: Woman's scarf, football, graduation picture, Bible, cross or picture of a cross.

Gospel truth: Because of Jesus' redemptive work and through the work of the Holy Spirit, we can experience peace.

Let me tell you a story about a little girl named Lizzie. Lizzie was three years old, and it was her first day of preschool. Mom took Lizzie to school, but when it was time to say good-bye, Lizzie cried because she knew she would miss her mom. So Lizzie's mom gave her something special to make Lizzie feel better. *Show the scarf.* Lizzie put her mom's scarf in a special place. When she felt lonely, she held it in her hand and thought about her mom. Then Lizzie felt better again.

Let me tell you a story about a 10-year-old boy named Dylan. Dylan was best friends with Tom. They loved to go fishing and play catch with the football. One day, Tom's family moved to a new town. When it was time for Tom and his dad to drive away, Dylan felt very sad. He knew he would really miss Tom. But Tom gave his friend something special to make him feel better. *Show the football.* Dylan put Tom's football in a special place. When he missed his friend, he would take out the football and think about Tom. Then Dylan felt better again.

Let me tell you a story about Mrs. Mason. She had a daughter who went away to college. The college was so far away that her daughter would only be able to come home to visit once in awhile. When it was time for her daughter to go away, Mrs. Mason hugged her and cried. She would miss her daughter so much. But her daughter gave her something special. *Show the graduation picture.* When Mrs. Mason missed her daughter, she would look at the picture and think about her. Then Mrs. Mason felt better again.

In today's Gospel lesson, Jesus is getting ready to die on the cross. He knows that He will rise again and go back to His Father in heaven. He knows that His friends, the disciples, will miss Him. So Jesus tells His disciples that He will give them something special. He will give them the Holy Spirit and the gift of peace. He gives the same gifts to you and to me.

When we were baptized, we received the gift of the Holy Spirit who created faith in Jesus in our hearts. The Holy Spirit also helps us feel the special kind of peace that Jesus gives to us. Peace is not something that we can look at like a scarf, a football, or a picture. Instead, peace is something that we feel in our hearts.

Hold up the Bible. When we listen to God's Word, peace is what we feel when we know that Jesus loves us and He will always be with us. *Hold up the cross.* When we look at a cross, peace is what we feel when we know that Jesus loves us so much that He died and rose again for us. Jesus gives us the gift of peace because He wants us to think about Him and know that He loves us. Someday we will live forever with Jesus in heaven. That will be the gift that will last forever.

Prayer: Dear Jesus, grant us the gift of peace through the Holy Spirit. Help us know that the more we learn about Your love, the more we will feel peace in our hearts. Amen.

Making the Best Choices

SEVENTH SUNDAY OF EASTER:
John 7:20–26

Text: Stop judging by mere appearances, and make a right judgment. *John 7:24*

Teaching aids: A bowl, a large spoon, a box marked "Ingredients," a Bible. In the box, put salt, flour, an egg, sugar, and vinegar.

Gospel truth: God forgives us for our poor choices through the redemptive work of Jesus, but we must accept responsibility for checking our choices against the criteria in the Bible.

Take out the bowl, spoon, and box. I am so glad you are all here today. I'm hungry for some brownies, so I thought I would make them for us. There are so many different ingredients in this box that I'm not sure what to choose. Oh well, I'm sure it won't make a difference which ones I choose.

Pour some sugar and flour into the bowl without measuring. Sugar and flour seem like good choices. *Add some vinegar and salt.* Next we'll add some salt and vinegar. *Stir everything together.* Hmmm! I bet I need an egg. *Add the egg without breaking the shell. Hum while you mix.*

This doesn't look like it will make very good brownies. What do you think? *Show the mixture to the children.* I wonder what I did wrong. I must have chosen the wrong ingredients. But how would I know the right ingredients to choose? *Let the children respond.* You're right! I need a recipe to make the right choices. If I follow what the recipe says, my brownies will turn out just right.

That reminds me of other choices you and I make each day. There is no recipe for us to follow to tell us what to do. I wonder how we will know what choices to make. For example, what if my best friend wants me to cheat on a test? How will I know what to do? *Let the children respond.* You are right! If I read the Bible, I will know that it is wrong to cheat. The Bible helps me to make the right choice.

What if my dad tells me it's too close to dinner so I can't take a cookie. I listen to what my dad says, but I am really hungry. Should I take the cookie or wait until dinner? How will I know what to do? *Let the children respond.* You are right! If I read the Bible, I will know that it is wrong to disobey my parents. The Bible helps me to make the right choice.

Sometimes, though, we make the wrong choices. That's when we sin. We might decide to listen to our friends instead of listening to the words from the Bible. God knows that we will make the wrong choices sometimes. That's why He sent Jesus to be our Savior. Because Jesus died on the cross and rose again, we are forgiven for our sins and all the bad choices we make.

We still need to try our best to make the right choices because we love Jesus and are thankful for what He has done for us. *Hold up the Bible.* That's why it is important to learn so much about the Bible. It's a little like having a recipe that will help us make the best brownies ever. When we know about the Bible, we will make the best choice of all. The most important thing for us is that we trust in Jesus, then we can ask Him to help us follow His commandments.

Prayer: God, You sent Jesus to be our Savior, and we know that You will forgive us when we make the wrong choices. Help us make the right choices by learning about Your love in the Bible. Amen.

"Spirit-ual" Souvenirs

—=◆◆◆=—

PENTECOST:
John 15:26–27; 16:4b–11

Text: "When the Counselor [the Holy Spirit] comes, whom I will send to you from the Father, the Spirit of truth who goes out from the Father, He will testify about Me. *John 15:26*

Teaching aids: A souvenir of some kind, preferably one that has a personal story behind it.

Gospel truth: The Holy Spirit is at work in the church, reminding God's children of the continuing presence of Jesus among us.

Show and briefly tell the story of a personal souvenir. The following is an example that you can adapt. When I was a little boy, my dad took a trip to New York City. When he returned, he brought me this little metal replica of the Empire State Building as a souvenir. *Show the souvenir.* I have kept it all these years.

He brought me the souvenir because he wanted me to know that the Empire State Building was an important place. He wanted me to know that he had been there. He wanted me to be able to see it for myself someday. Until I saw it for myself, this little statue was a reminder of what it would be like to be there. Now I have been to New York City myself. I've seen the Empire State Building, but I keep this souvenir because it reminds me of my dad and our relationship. Souvenirs are like that—they help us remember places.

They help us remember the *people* who are important to us.

Forty days after rising from the dead, Jesus went to be with His Father in heaven. He knew that we would not be able to see Him anymore, so Jesus sent the Holy Spirit to remind us that He loves us, that He is always with us, and that soon we will join Him in heaven. You might say that the Holy Spirit does that work of reminding us about Jesus through souvenirs—real things that we can touch and see. They remind us of the presence and power of Jesus. Let me point out some of those "souvenirs" that we see every week.

Point to or gather around the baptismal font. We could call this baptismal font a "souvenir" of Jesus. Whenever someone is baptized, Jesus is at work among us, forgiving sins and opening heaven for a new believer.

Point to or gather around the altar. Or, show the bread and wine of Holy Communion. We could call these elements of bread and wine "souvenirs" of Jesus. When the people of God receive Holy Communion, Jesus is at work among us, forgiving sins and opening heaven for believers.

Point to the pulpit and/or show a Bible. When the Word of God is read among us, when you are taught by your pastor or teachers to know and love Jesus, when someone comes to faith in Christ, then Jesus is at work among us, opening heaven, forgiving sins, and pointing us to our heavenly home with God the Father.

Today is Pentecost, the "birthday" of the church. It is a day when we celebrate that Jesus, through the Holy Spirit, has been at work among us for another year. We cannot actually see Him, but the "souvenirs" that the Holy Spirit keeps before our eyes remind us of our Lord and encourage us to begin this new year with courage and confidence and joy in the presence and the power of Jesus among us.

Prayer: O God, through Your Holy Spirit, help us "see" Jesus, believe in Him, and follow Him as faithful servants and disciples. Amen.

It's the Truth

THE HOLY TRINITY:
John 16:12–15

Text: "When He, the Spirit of truth, comes, He will guide you into all truth." *John 16:13*

Teaching aids: Your hands and arms and an enthusiastic attitude. You also may want to have pictures of common symbols for the three persons of the Trinity.

Gospel truth: God is at work in the world as Father, Son, and Holy Spirit. Unable to fully comprehend this mystery, the church is still moved to praise.

Let me tell you three things about God that we know from the Bible to be absolutely true—three things that the whole Christian church celebrates this day—three things that help us know, love, and trust God completely. Those three things are: God is Father, God is Jesus, God is Spirit. Here's a way to remember these three truths.

When I think of God the Father, my left hand goes up in the air. Please raise yours with me. *Raise your left hand or, if you are facing the children, your right hand to provide a mirror-image for them to imitate. Hold your hand high as you continue.* My left hand is nearest my heart, and that reminds me that God is a lover. He loved us from the beginning of time. He loved us enough to send His Son, Jesus, to pay the penalty for our sins. The church is so excited about that truth that it "cheers" the Father with the very special word *alleluia.* When I say, "God is Father," you respond with a loud "Alleluia!" Let's try it. *Do the cheer: God is Father! Alleluia!*

When I think of Jesus, my right hand goes in the air.

Please raise yours with me. *Raise your right hand or, if you are facing the children, your left hand to provide a mirror-image for them to imitate. Hold your hand high as you continue.* My right hand reminds me that Jesus is God the Father's "right-hand man." A "right-hand man" gets the work done. He can be depended on to carry out whatever assignment is given him. Jesus is the one who got God's work of love and forgiveness done in the world. He got it done on the cross when He died to pay for our sins. He got it done when He rose from the dead on Easter. Then He went to "sit at God's right hand" as we say in our creed. He continues to get God's love-work done through the Holy Spirit. The church is so excited about that truth that it "cheers" Jesus with the very special word *alleluia*. When I say, "God is Jesus," you respond with a loud "Alleluia!" Let's try it. *Do the cheer: God is Jesus. Alleluia!*

When I think of the Holy Spirit, both hands go in the air. Please raise yours with me. *Raise both hands in the air.* My hands in the air remind me that the Holy Spirit made His presence known on Pentecost with tongues of fire on the disciples' heads and with the rush of wind. *Wiggle your fingers behind your head to indicate the flames. Wave both hands above your head for the wind.* The truth is that although we cannot see the Holy Spirit, it is the Spirit who prepares our hearts and minds to receive the love of God in Jesus. The Spirit is the way Jesus is always with us. He brings us into contact with Jesus. He works faith in our hearts and lives. He guides and teaches us to praise God as Father, Son, and Spirit. The church is so excited about this truth that it "cheers" the Spirit with the very special word *alleluia*. When I say, "God is Spirit," you respond with a loud "Alleluia!" Let's try it. *Do the cheer: God is Spirit. Alleluia!*

Now let's put this all together in a "three-in-one" cheer. Perhaps the whole congregation will join us as we call out our "alleluia!"

God is Father! Alleluia!

God is Jesus! Alleluia!

God is Spirit! Alleluia!

Praise the Lord! Alleluia!

That's the truth of the Holy Trinity. We may not ever completely understand it, but it is always the subject of our prayer and praise.

Prayer: Gracious and loving God, Father, Son, and Holy Spirit, we praise You for Your love, for Your forgiveness, and for Your work in and through us. Teach us to love You and serve You in return and to share the good news of salvation with others. Amen.

Jesus, Heal Us

⟾⬥⟾

SECOND SUNDAY AFTER PENTECOST:
Luke 7:1–10

Text: Say the word, and my servant will be healed. … Jesus said, "I tell you, I have not found such a faith even in Israel." *Luke 7:7, 9*

Teaching aids: Things doctors use to help people: stethoscope, syringe, empty medicine bottle, bandage.

Gospel truth: Jesus is the source of all healing. Faith in Him removes even the fatal malady of sin and death.

Here are some things doctors use to help people who are sick or hurt. *Hold up each item as you talk about it.* Here's a stethoscope, a bottle of medicine, a syringe, and a bandage. They are a doctor's tools of healing. If you fell off your bicycle and broke your arm, you would rush to the doctor so she could heal your arm. People usually do what their doctor tells them. We listen to doctors and follow their directions because we believe that our doctors want us to be healthy. We really believe that they know what to do to help us get better when we are sick or hurt.

Today's Gospel is about a captain in the Roman army who asked Jesus to heal his servant and friend. He believed with all his heart that Jesus had the power to heal his servant. He believed that all Jesus had to do was say a healing word and the servant would be well. Jesus was amazed at the man's belief—his faith—and Jesus did heal the captain's servant, using only the power of His word.

Jesus wants us to be free of pain and sickness, and sometimes He heals people just as he did the Roman captain's servant. But Jesus is always concerned about a more important sickness—the sickness of sin. The way He takes away the sickness of sin is not with pills or stethoscopes or bandages or shots. Jesus heals us from our sin by His death on the cross. Jesus used the cross to heal our broken relationship with God. And Jesus wants us to do the same thing. He wants us to use His cross to help Him heal other people. When we forgive other people in Jesus' name, we are helping them with the healing Word of God.

Some of you may one day be doctors or nurses, helping to heal people from their physical sicknesses. But all of you, right now, are asked by Jesus to spread the "healing" of the Gospel with the simple words: God forgives you, and I forgive you.

Prayer: Dear Lord God, we pray for all who need healing from illness, pain, and suffering. We pray that You would, for Jesus' sake, forgive our sins and the sins of all who believe in You that we might live free from all suffering, illness, and sinfulness with You in heaven forever. Amen.

Jesus Changes Things

—=◆=—

THIRD SUNDAY AFTER PENTECOST:
Luke 7:11–17

Text: "When the Lord saw her [the widow], His heart went out to her and He said, 'Don't cry.' " *Luke 7:13*

Teaching aids: A large, round poster (preferably on a stick or pole) with a happy face on one side and a sad face on the other side.

Gospel truth: God's love in Jesus reverses all our human expectations. Sorrow is turned to joy, despair is turned to hope, and death is turned to life.

Briefly tell the stories of the widow of Zarephath and the widow of Nain. Rotate the happy and sad faces of the poster as you make the good news/bad news distinctions. Rotation spots are indicated by the words "happy" and "sad" in parentheses. (If your congregation does not read the Old Testament lesson, 1 Kings 17:17–24, adapt the following to present only the Gospel lesson.)

Today's Bible readings tell about two sad *(sad)* women. Both had experienced death in their families. Each woman had been married. *(happy)* But each of their husbands died. *(sad)* Each of the women had wonderful sons. *(happy)* But each of their sons died. *(sad)* Each had hearts filled with hope *(happy)* for the future when their families were alive. But after their husbands and their sons died, they were hopeless. *(sad)* They were very sad. Not only had they lost people they loved, they were also without anyone who could provide and care for them.

But God came into the life of each widow to turn her sorrow *(sad)* into joy *(happy)* and her despair *(sad)* into hope. *(happy)* In the Old Testament story, God answered the prayer of His prophet Elijah and restored life to the dead boy. In the Gospel story, Jesus Himself touched the body of the widow's son and brought him back to life. It became a happy time for the widows. God had taken the frown *(sad)* of sadness from their faces and replaced it with a smile *(happy)* of joy.

We are told these stories in the Bible to teach us that God has conquered the power of death. *(sad)* He wants life *(happy)* for us. People do die *(sad)* and God does not bring everyone who dies back to life on this earth. But He does promise that everyone who believes in Jesus will have eternal life. *(happy)* That means that we do not have to be afraid of dying. In fact, many people who believe in Jesus smile at death. They know that, for the Christian, earthly death is the way to be with God in heaven forever. And while we may be sad *(sad)* when someone we love and care for is no longer with us on earth, we also rejoice, *(happy)* knowing that anyone who knows Jesus as Savior is on the way to heaven. Death can't stop a Christian.

Prayer: Dear Jesus, fill us with the joy of Your salvation. Help us not to fear death but to rejoice in Your promise of eternal life in heaven. While we are here on earth, teach us to help and comfort those who are threatened by death and to always spread the good news of Your love and promise. Amen.

Bridging the Gap
(or The Bridge of Faith)

———⫸◆⫷———

FOURTH SUNDAY AFTER PENTECOST:
Luke 7:36–50

Text: Jesus said to her, "Your sins are forgiven." The other guests began to say among themselves, "Who is this who even forgives sins?" Jesus said to the woman, "Your faith has saved you; go in peace." *Luke 7:48–50*

Teaching aids: Two pictures of "gaps" that have been overcome. One could be a bridge over a large body of water. One could be a boat crossing a large body of water. (Optional: two stacks of hymnals and a cross)

Gospel truth: The gap between heaven and earth caused by our sinfulness is spanned forever by the cross of Christ.

Look at this first picture. *Show the picture of the bridge.* These two points of land are separated by a giant hole, which we might call a "gap." How would you get from one side of this "gap" to the other? *Let the children respond.* You mean you would cross over that bridge? Do you think it would support you? Do you believe it wouldn't fall? In this picture it seems that the only way to get from one side to the other is to cross the bridge. There is no other way, and if you wanted to get across this gap, you would have to trust that the bridge would get you there.

Look at this second picture. *Show the picture of the boat.* What if you wanted to get from one side of this body of water to the other? The water fills a great "gap" between the two points of land. It's too far to swim, so what would you do? *Let the children respond.* That's right, you would take the boat. But boats seem like such clumsy things. Do you believe a boat like this could get you from one side to the other? Really? In this picture it seems that the only way to get from one side to the other is to take the boat. There is no other way, and if you wanted to get across, you would have to trust that the boat would get you there.

We are separated from God by sin. You could say that there is a great "gap" between heaven and earth. *To demonstrate, show two stacks of hymnals and use the cross to bridge them as you explain.* We cannot get to God or into His heaven on our own. There is really only one way to get to God, and that is through His Son, Jesus. Jesus died on the cross so that our sins would be forgiven, and forgiveness is the only way to "bridge the gap" between God and us. When we trust in Jesus for forgiveness, we can be sure that we will get across the "gap" of sin and into the presence of God.

Faith is another word for trust. The woman in today's Gospel reading knew that she needed to believe in Jesus if she was to be healed. Jesus praised her for her great faith. We trust that a bridge will hold our weight and that a boat will not sink, but we can be wrong; bridges sometimes do collapse and boats sometimes do sink. But when we have faith in Jesus, and we trust Him for the forgiveness of our sins, we are never disappointed. Jesus is the way we get to God the Father. Jesus is the way we "bridge the gap" between earth and heaven.

Prayer: Heavenly Father, send us Your Holy Spirit to give us faith to trust in Jesus for the forgiveness of our sins. Teach us by Your Spirit to know that we will be spending eternity in heaven with You. In the name of Jesus. Amen.

Give Me
J-E-S-U-S

———≫•◇•≪———

FIFTH SUNDAY AFTER PENTECOST:
Luke 9:18–24

Text: "But what about you?" [Jesus] asked. "Who do you say that I am?" *Luke 9:20*

Teaching aids: Large individual cards or posters with the letters J-E-S-U-S on them. They can be put on easels, taped to the wall, or held by individual children. Also a single card or sheet of paper with all the letters on it should be prepared as a "take-home" item.

Gospel truth: Empowered by God's Spirit to confess the Christ, the disciple of Jesus gladly takes on the task of making His name and work known to others.

In today's Gospel reading, Jesus' disciple, Peter, makes a confession. He says what he believes to be true about Jesus: that Jesus is the Messiah or, as Peter says it, "the Christ of God."

Disciples need to be able to talk about their master, to say what is true about Him so that others might be convinced to follow Him too. I am a follower of Jesus, and I believe you are all followers of Jesus too. As I was thinking of some ways we could practice talking about Him to ourselves and to others, I thought of using the letters of Jesus' name to say some things that are true about Him.

Hold up the "J" card. Give me a "J!" "J" is for Joy. Because He forgives my sins and promises me heaven, Jesus brings joy into my life. I can be a joyful person because I know that, for Jesus' sake, God loves me.

Hold up the "E" card. Give me an "E!" "E" is for Eternal. Because I know my sins are forgiven, I know that I will have eternal life. That means that I am sure that I will be living with Jesus in heaven forever.

Hold up the "S" card. Give me an "S!" "S" is for Servant. Being a follower of Jesus means that I am a servant of God and of other people in His name. I don't have to figure out on my own how to be a servant, Jesus is my model. His life is my example.

Hold up the "U" card. Give me a "U!" "U" is for Unlimited Love. There is no end to God's love for me because of Jesus. As His disciple, my job is to keep loving others in the same way Jesus loves me.

Hold up the "S" card. Give me an "S!" "S" is for Savior. Jesus is the only one who can rescue us from the power of sin and death. As a follower of Jesus, that is the main thing I should tell other people about Him.

Before you go today, I will give you a piece of paper with these letters on it. During the week, work with your parents and other people in your family to find other words that can help you say who Jesus is and what He does. One of the most important jobs of a disciple is to be able to talk to others about Jesus. If you see me during the week, tell me about some of the words you discovered, or show me your list next Sunday. As you work on this project, know that the Holy Spirit is at work in you, because you can't talk about Jesus without the Spirit's help.

Prayer: Dear God, let your Holy Spirit teach us about our Lord Jesus. Then give us the wisdom and the courage to confess Him as our Lord. Make us Your bold and confident disciples, for Jesus sake. Amen.

First Things First

SIXTH SUNDAY AFTER PENTECOST:
Luke 9:51–62

Text: "I will follow You wherever You go." *Luke 9:57b*

Teaching aids: Bible, toothbrush, telephone, wrapped candy, ball, construction paper cut into the shape of the number 1 with a picture or sticker of Jesus attached (you may wish to make one for each child).

Gospel truth: As we follow Jesus, He helps us share God's love with all people.

Have you ever heard someone say, "First things first?" I was thinking about those words the other day. I began wondering what "first things" might be. *Show the toothbrush.* When you brush your teeth, what is the first thing you do? *Show the telephone.* When you call someone on the telephone, what is the first thing you do? *Hold up the candy.* When you want to eat a piece of candy, what is the first thing you do? *Show the ball.* When you want to catch a ball, what is the first thing you do? *As each question is asked, allow time for the children to respond.*

I also began to wonder what would happen if you skipped the first thing and did the second thing first. *Show each item as you discuss it.* When you brush your teeth, what would happen if you skipped the first thing *(as named by the children)* and did the second thing first? When you call someone on the phone, what would happen if you began by doing the second thing? When you eat a piece of candy, what would happen if you skipped the first thing and did the second thing first? *Allow time for the children to respond.* Beginning with the second thing doesn't work!

Our Bible verse for today says, "I will follow You wherever You go." When you follow someone, what is the first thing you do? You set aside what you want to do and follow that person. It is very difficult to keep on doing what you're doing and to follow someone else. *Choose two children to play catch. Direct them to continue their game and follow what you do. Begin an action for the children to follow— one that cannot be followed if they continue to play catch.*

When we follow Jesus, the first thing we must do is stop what we're doing so that we can really follow Him. Jesus tells us to put everything else aside to follow Him and "proclaim the kingdom of God" to all people.

Show the number 1. Following Jesus and sharing His love with others is number 1—the first thing. When we keep the second, third, and fourth things in their places and make Jesus first, everything in our lives begins to have order and meaning. First things are the most important things. Following Jesus and sharing His love is the most important thing we can ever do and He, as our leader, will help us.

Prayer: Dear Jesus, thank You for inviting us to follow You and to share Your love with other people. Teach us to follow. Show us Your way. Help us to make You first in our lives. In Your name we pray. Amen.

I Can

SEVENTH SUNDAY AFTER PENTECOST: Luke 10:1–12, 16

Text: The harvest is plentiful, but the workers are few. Ask the Lord of the harvest, therefore, to send out workers into His harvest field. *Luke 10:2*

Teaching aids: A Bible, poster board or chart paper imprinted with the word *can*. Print the letter "t" (so it resembles a cross) on a separate sheet of paper and tape it at the end of the word *can*, so it can easily be removed.

Gospel truth: Our Lord will provide people and give them the gifts they need to proclaim the good news of His saving love.

Have you ever said the words "I can't!" *Point to the word "can't."* Sometimes when things are a little bit difficult or when it is something we have never done before, we find it safer to say, "I can't do it" than to try and maybe make a mistake.

There are many people who don't know the good news that Jesus loves them and that He died on the cross and rose again for them. Jesus needs workers—people like you and me to tell others about His great love. *Read today's text from the Bible.* We can pray that our Lord sends workers to share the good news of our Savior Jesus Christ and we can be His workers ourselves.

When Jesus says, "Work for Me," what will your answer be? Let's look at the word *can't.* Do you see the cross at the end of the word? *Remove the "t" and place it above the word "can."* The cross of Christ turns our "I can't" into "I can" when we focus on it first! Jesus wants us to be workers for Him, telling all others about His love. We can trust Him (*point to the cross*) to help us do the job!

Let's practice. When I point to you, you say, "With His help, I know I can!" and point to the cross.

When Jesus said, "Follow Me," to Him I quickly ran. *Point to the children.*

With His help I know I can! *Point to the cross.*

He wants me to go and serve that woman and that man. *Point to the children.*

With His help I know I can! *Point to the cross.*

My Jesus says, "Put Me first, you know I am your Man!" *Point to the children.*

With His help I know I can! *Point to the cross.*

Jesus says, "Work for Me, I have the very best plan!" *Point to the children.*

With His help I know I can! *Point to the cross.*

Prayer: Dear Jesus, We thank and praise You for choosing us to be workers for You. Help us to trust that You will help us with what You ask us to do. Turn our "can't dos" into "can dos." In Your name we pray. Amen.

The Love Job

EIGHTH SUNDAY AFTER PENTECOST:
Luke 10:25–37

Text: "Love the Lord your God with all your heart and with all your soul and with all your strength and with all your mind; and, love your neighbor as yourself." *Luke 10:27*

Teaching aids: A Bible, pictures or illustrations of each of the following: eyes, ears, mouths, feet, and hands; chart paper or tag board divided into five columns; a large paper cross; chart holder; masking tape.

Gospel truth: God sent Jesus to live, die, and rise so that one day we can live with Him in eternity. Our response to His great love is to give our love and service to Him and to all people.

Letting others know that you love them is important. Can you name some ways that you can let others know that you love them? *As children offer suggestions, place corresponding pictures at the top of the chart, one in each column. Add any remaining pictures, offering suggestions as to their use: ears for listening to others, mouths for saying "I love you," hands and feet for doing kind and helpful things, eyes for seeing the needs of others.*

Read today's text from the Bible. God gave us some wonderful tools to show our love to others and to Him. He gave us our eyes, ears, mouths, hands, and feet to show love. How can we use these things *(point to the pictures)* to show our love to God? *Write the children's responses in the appropriate columns.* Showing love to God means showing love to others also. But some people are mean and there are some people we just don't like very much. And sometimes we have so many things that we want to do, that we don't take the time to do things other people need to have done. Sometimes we'd just rather have other people do things for us. That's kind of selfish, isn't it?

God's love always has time for others. God's love puts the needs of others first. God's love doesn't ask, "Does he deserve it?" Or, "What's in it for me?" God's love doesn't say, "They do bad things, why should I love them?" God's love is just because He loves us. God's love is so great that He sent His only Son to die for us so that through the life, death, and resurrection of Jesus we can one day live with Him forever in heaven. God's love is *Grace*—love that isn't deserved or earned. God's love is the greatest love of all and God wants us to show everyone that same kind of love.

How can we show God's kind of love? We're only human, after all! God knows that loving others can be very difficult for us, so He sent Jesus to show us how. *Tape the cross over the chart.*

We simply need to learn about what Jesus did and then in every situation ask ourselves, "What would Jesus do?" When we love others the way Jesus did, we can use the "equipment" God has given us—*(point to the chart pictures)* our eyes, ears, hands, feet, and mouths—to do the love job.

Prayer: Thank You for loving me so much that You sent Your only Son to live, die, and rise to life for me. Guide me to use the gifts You have given me to do Your "love job" so that in all I do and say I praise Your gracious name. In the name of Jesus I pray. Amen.

Minutes for Jesus

NINTH SUNDAY AFTER PENTECOST:
Luke 10:18–42

Text: Mary has chosen what is better, and it will not be taken away from her. *Luke 10:42*

Teaching aids: A working clock with a second hand or a stopwatch.

Gospel truth: The coming of Christ is God's gift to all people. We have only to take the time to celebrate His presence among us by giving our undivided attention to His Word, so we are equipped to serve as His ambassadors in the world.

Have you ever started to speak and had the person you want to talk with say, "Wait a minute." Let's find out how long a minute is. *Watch the second hand on the clock or set the stopwatch for one minute.* A minute can seem very long when you are anxious to tell someone something or when you need that person's help. How do you feel when someone says, "Wait a minute?" *Let the children respond.*

Briefly tell the story of Mary and Martha. Martha, in her own way, was working to serve Jesus. The problem wasn't her preparation of the meal. It was that she was troubled and anxious about many things. If we take time to put Jesus first, we can go about our other tasks without being troubled or anxious.

Mary's minutes with Jesus were very important and Jesus wanted her to have that time with Him. Mary put all the other important things in her life aside to listen to what Jesus had to say. She knew that by giving Jesus her minutes, she could do everything else in an even better way—His way.

Sometimes we get so busy that we say, "Wait a minute" to Jesus. How do you suppose that makes Him feel? Do you know that each minute is one that we can never ever get back again. We can use our minutes wisely and set some of them aside to learn more about Jesus and His great love for us. We can use some of our minutes to talk with Him in prayer and to sing praises to Him. We can even use some of our minutes to help other people in a way that He would want.

There are 1,440 minutes in a day and 10,080 minutes in a week. How much time is a minute? *Watch the second hand or set the stop watch for one minute.* A minute can be a lot of time for listening or not listening to the words of Jesus. How many minutes can you give to Jesus?

Prayer: Dear Jesus, thank You for giving us Your Word so that we can learn more about You and grow in our faith. Help us to choose to give our time to You in prayer and praise and in reading and hearing Your Word. In Your name we pray. Amen.

Prayer Practice

TENTH SUNDAY AFTER PENTECOST:
Luke 11:1–13

Text: "Lord, teach us to pray." *Luke 11:1b*

Teaching aids: A Bible, project directions and project pieces, tools that are obviously not suitable for the project, chart paper.

Gospel truth: God encourages us to come to Him boldly and persistently in prayer, and He promises to listen when we pray.

I have a project that I am trying to do. I brought the directions, hoping that perhaps you could help me. *Read the directions in their entirety and then fold them up and put them away.* Now, where do I begin? *Allow time for the children to assist you. If tools are required, admit that you didn't bring the correct ones.* I guess I'm going to have to spend more time on this. Maybe if I reread the directions and get the right tools, I'll be able to assemble this more easily. I guess if I had more practice at this, it would be easier for me.

Once, Jesus' disciples wanted to learn to pray. Prayer was something they didn't know how to do. They needed directions from Jesus. The disciples said to Jesus, "Lord, teach us to pray." Jesus taught His disciples and all of us exactly how to pray. He gave us the tools—the words—to say and to use in all of our prayers. We must follow His directions and practice praying, if we are to know how to pray and for what to pray. *Read Luke 11:2–13.*

The prayer we know as The Lord's Prayer is Jesus' "directions" for praying. The prayer teaches us to praise God and to come to God with our needs and the needs of others. The directions for praying, according to Jesus, are *(write the directions on chart paper)*: 1) Begin prayer by praising God for the wonderful things that only He can do. 2) Come to God when we or others need His help.

Our cry for help is "Lord, have mercy." Mercy is a special word. It means undeserved kindness and it is a blessing from God the Father.

Let's practice praying according to the directions Jesus gave us. Each time I make the sign of the cross with my fingers *(demonstrate by overlapping index fingers to make the shape of a cross)* you say the words "Lord, have mercy."

Prayer: (An adaptation of Psalm 86)

You are mighty and do wonderful things; You alone are God.

Lord, have mercy.

Listen to me, Lord, and answer me, because I am helpless.

Lord, have mercy.

You are my God; I pray to You all day long.

Lord, have mercy.

You are good to me and You forgive me.

Lord, have mercy.

Your love never ends for all who pray to You.

Lord, have mercy.

I call to You in times of trouble, because You answer my prayer.

Lord, have mercy.

Teach me, Lord, what You want me to do, and I will obey You faithfully.

Lord, have mercy.

I will praise You with my whole heart and tell everyone of Your greatness! Amen.

More! More! More!

ELEVENTH SUNDAY AFTER PENTECOST: Luke 12:13–21

Text: A man's life does not consist in the abundance of his possessions. *Luke 12:15b*

Teaching aids: An empty ice cream container; candy (one piece for each child); a piece of clothing; a cross.

Gospel truth: God's gift of the Savior enables us to focus on how we honor God and serve His people, rather than on what we own or how much we have.

Tell the following short stories. Instruct the children to say the words "More! More! More!" each time they hear the phrase beginning "It's not fair ..."

Once there were two brothers. Their father said to them, "Sons, I brought home a container of ice cream *(show the ice cream container)* for you to share." Then turning to the oldest son he said, "Please scoop the ice cream into two bowls." When the ice cream had been scooped into the bowls, the older son gave a bowl to his younger brother. Comparing the two bowls of ice cream, the younger son said, "It's not fair, he has **More! More! More!**"

A group of friends were gathered around a piñata filled with candy treats *(hold up the candy)*. Batting it with a long stick, they soon broke a hole in the piñata. The children scrambled to gather the candy that poured from the hole. When all of the candy had been collected, the children compared the amount each had. One of the children cried, "It's not fair, you have **More! More! More!**"

A brother and sister each took a turn to go shopping for new clothes *(hold up clothing)* with their mother. The boy had chosen a pair of pants and a shirt, both of which he needed. His sister chose a sweater and shirt, pants, and a matching pair of socks, all of which she needed. When the boy saw what his mother had purchased for his sister, he turned to her and said, "It's not fair, she got **More! More! More!**"

Have you ever said the words "It's not fair" because you felt someone received more than you did? *Let the children respond.* Once a man came to Jesus and wanted Jesus to make the man's brother give him half of what the brother owned. Jesus said to the man, "Watch out! Be on your guard against all kinds of greed." Then He reminded the man that life is not about how much we own, but rather how much we give to God and people. *Show the cross.* Jesus' life, death, and resurrection enables us to focus on what is most important—praising God and serving others, rather than on how much we have or own.

Prayer: Lord Jesus Christ, we ask Your forgiveness for the times that we want more of the things in our world. Help us to focus on You, praising Your name and serving others. Amen.

My Promise Jar

TWELFTH SUNDAY AFTER PENTECOST:
Luke 12:32–40

Text: "Do not be afraid, little flock, for your Father has been pleased to give you the kingdom." *Luke 12:32*

Teaching aids: A Bible, a clear unbreakable jar with a lid (Label the jar "My Worry Jar." Make a second label that reads "My Promise Jar."); slips of blank paper, cellophane tape.

Gospel truth: God promises to provide for all of our needs, especially our need for forgiveness through Jesus.

Are you a worrier? *Show the jar and read the label.* Have you ever been afraid or worried? *Let the children respond.* I know I've been afraid. *Name some of your worries and fears. Write them on the slips of paper and put them one by one in the jar. Write down some of the worries and fears the children named and add them to the jar.*

One thing that helps us deal with our worries and fears is to write them down and then set aside "worry time" each day to think about those things. The "worry time" is the only time each day that we allow ourselves to think about what makes us anxious or afraid.

Can you think of another way we can deal with the things that cause us to worry and be afraid? *Let the children respond.* We can give our worries to our heavenly Father. *Open the Bible to Luke 12:32.* He tells us in today's lesson, "Do not be afraid, little flock, for your Father has been pleased to give you the kingdom."

We cannot see God, so how can we make our worries

and fears His? We can talk to Him about anything that is bothering us. God promises to listen. Our worries and fears may not disappear. The difficult things in our lives may not go away, but when we share them with our Lord, He will help us handle them. Knowing this, we can remove each of these items from the "worry jar" and place them in a "promise jar." *Cover the "worry" label with the "promise" label. Then reread the printed slips, using them to pray a litany.*

Prayer:
When we are troubled by *(read a worry or fear)*,
Remind us of Your love and care.
When we are troubled by *(read a worry or fear)*,
Remind us of Your love and care.
In the name of Jesus we pray. **Amen.**

Getting It
Over With

THIRTEENTH SUNDAY AFTER PENTECOST: Luke 12:49–53

Text: But I have a baptism to undergo, and how distressed I am until it is completed. *Luke 12:50*

Teaching aids: Appointment card; two pieces of poster board: On one piece of poster board draw a cross, along with the words *Jesus* and *Good Friday.* On the other card, write the words *God* and *The Last Day.*

Gospel truth: Jesus knew of the suffering and death that lay ahead of Him.

Do you know what an appointment card is? *Show appointment card.* Appointment is a big word that grownups use when they have to be at a certain place at a certain time. Sometimes they have little cards like this to remind them when and where they have to be. My card says that I have to be at *(fill in where you have to be)* on *(fill in your appointment date).*

Can you think of a time when you have to be at a certain place at a certain time to keep an appointment? You might have to go get your hair cut, see the dentist, have a yearly checkup at the doctor's office, or have a picture taken with your family for the church directory. Even a birthday party can be a kind of appointment. So can coming to church every Sunday. These are all things we have to do at a certain place at a certain time or we will miss them.

Do you like to go to all the appointment places I just

mentioned? Why or why not? *Let the children respond.*
Some appointments are fun to go to, some are not. Sometimes the only good thing about going to an appointment is when it is over.

Have your ever heard someone say he wants to get it over with? Do you know what that means? It means that he has to do something he doesn't like to do, so he wants to hurry and get it finished so he doesn't have to worry about it anymore. Have you ever had to do something that you just wanted to get it over with? *Let the children respond.*

Show card with cross and words "Jesus" and "Good Friday." This big "appointment card" reminds us that Jesus once had something special He had to do at a certain place at a certain time. What does the cross on our card remind us of? *Let the children respond.* The cross reminds us of the cross Jesus died on. The words *Good Friday* tell us the day Jesus died. Jesus had an appointment to die on the cross on the first Good Friday.

In our Gospel reading today, Jesus talks about His coming suffering and death on the cross. The thought of this made Him sad. Why? Jesus knew it would be hard to die on the cross.

Do you look forward to having to do something you know will hurt you? *Let the children respond.* No you don't, and neither do I. Yet in the Gospel reading Jesus says that He will be unhappy until His death on the cross is finished. Since it had to be done, Jesus wanted it to be done quickly.

Why did Jesus want to suffer and die for us? Because He loves us. He knew that dying on the cross was the only way to make up for our sins. He knew that this was the only way for us to live with Him in heaven.

Show card with words "God" and "The Last Day." Someday you will have an important appointment, the most important one you will ever have. It will be with God on the Last Day, the day Jesus comes to take His children to heaven.

And we don't need to be afraid of this appointment

because Jesus kept His Good Friday appointment on the cross. Jesus' death on the cross has taken away all our sins. We can face God on the Last Day without being afraid. Because of Jesus' death on the cross, we will live with Jesus forever in heaven. That's an appointment to look forward to.

Prayer: Dear Jesus, thank You for loving us enough to suffer and die in our place. Thank You for forgiving our sins. Amen.

From All Directions

———◆———

FOURTEENTH SUNDAY AFTER PENTECOST:
Luke 13:22–30

Text: People will come from the east and the west and north and south, and will take their places at the feast in the kingdom of God. *Luke 13:29*

Teaching aids: Compass; a circle with the letters N, S, E, and W written around the outside and a cross in the center with arrows pointing from each end. Optional: Use a globe to show children the different places to which you refer.

Gospel truth: God calls people from all parts of the earth to live with Him in His heavenly kingdom.

Show compass. Today I brought a compass. Do you know how it is used? *Let the children respond.* It shows us the directions north, south, east, and west. Let's see where these directions are from where we are standing today. The arrow points to the direction north. *Let children watch as you move the compass to show the arrow pointing to N.* The letter N shows the direction north. Pretend that you are a compass and point to the north. *Lead children in pointing north with their arms.*

Now, let's look for the other directions. Here's W. It stands for west. Let's point to the west. *Lead the children in pointing to the west.* What do you think the E stands for? *Let the children respond.* The east, that's right. Let's point that direction. *Lead children in pointing east.* What about the letter S? What does it stand for? *Let the children respond.* Yes, it stands for the south. Let's point south. *Lead children in pointing south with their arms.*

In our Bible reading today, Jesus talked about people coming from all directions of the compass—north, south, east, and west—to take their places in God's heavenly kingdom. When He said this, Jesus was speaking to people living in the land of Israel, a country far to the east of us (*point to east*), far across the ocean.

Some of the people who lived in Jesus' time thought that only people like them, who lived where Jesus lived, would go to heaven. Jesus wanted to remind these people that God wanted people from all the directions—north, south, east, and west—to live with Him in heaven. *Point to four directions.*

Show circle with cross in the center. What did I draw on my circle that is the same as on a compass? *Let the children respond.* Yes, the letters N, S, E, and W. Do you remember what those letters stand for? *Point to the letters and have the children say the direction that corresponds with each letter.*

What is different about my circle? *Let the children respond.* The cross in the center and the arrows pointing out at each of the ends of the cross. What does the cross remind us of? *Let the children respond.* Yes, it reminds us of Jesus' death on the cross. Where do the arrows at the end of the cross point? *Let the children respond.* To the four directions: north, south, east, and west. The arrows of the cross point to all the directions where people live because Jesus came to save all people.

Can you think of some people from different parts of the world that Jesus came to save? *Let the children respond.* He came to save Eskimos from far north. *Point north.* He came to save African people far to the south. *Point to the south.* He came to save Chinese people far to the east. *Point east.* Jesus came to save people like us who live far to the west.

Point west.

Jesus came to bring people from all directions—north, south, east, and west—to live with Him in heaven. *Point to the four directions.* Jesus came so that all of us here today could go to heaven. *Point to children and the rest of the congregation.*

How does it make you feel to know that God wants you in His kingdom? It makes us feel very happy, doesn't it? How can we share this happiness? By telling others around us about Jesus so that someday they too will join Him in heaven.

Prayer: Thank You, God, for wanting all kinds of people to live in Your heavenly kingdom. Thank You for sending Jesus to die for our sins so that we can live with Him forever. Help us share this Good News with others. Amen.

How to Be "Something"

━━➤◆⟵━━

FIFTEENTH SUNDAY AFTER PENTECOST: Luke 14:1, 7–14

Text: For everyone who exalts himself will be humbled, and he who humbles himself will be exalted. *Luke 14:11*

Teaching aids: Paper bag (lunch-bag size), balloon

Gospel truth: Trust in God, not yourself, for salvation.

Sometimes we hear people say that someone thinks that he or she is "something." Do you know what it means for someone to think he is "something?" *Let the children respond.* It means he thinks he is really important, more important than other people.

Have you ever met children who think they are "something?" *Let the children respond.* They think they are the best in all the games they play. They think their toys are better than your toys. They may want to be "the boss" all the time, always telling you what to do when you play together. How do you feel when you play with someone who thinks she is "something"? *Let the children respond.* Sometimes children who think they are "something" make children playing with them feel they are "nothing."

Jesus once talked about some people who lived in His time who thought they were "something." He said, "Everyone who exalts himself will be humbled."

Let's use a paper bag to help us understand what Jesus meant. *Blow up a paper bag and hold the end.* To *exalt* yourself means to try to make yourself seem big and important. It means to think that you are "something."

What happens when someone keeps on telling everyone else that he is "something"? *Let the children respond.* You might believe him once or twice, but not all the time. Other children may not believe what he says about himself either. He is like a paper bag that gets too puffed up with a lot of hot air until suddenly it goes pop. *Pop the bag.*

Jesus said that those who exalt themselves, or think that they are "something," will be humbled. *Humbled* means made to see that they are not "something" after all. When Jesus said this, He was thinking about some people at His time who thought they were "something" in the eyes of God. They thought they were so good that they could get to heaven just by being good, without Jesus. Sometimes people today think the same thing.

Can we earn heaven by being good? *Let the children respond.* No. How do we get to heaven? *Let the children respond.* By faith in Jesus, who died to save us.

When the Last Day comes, these people will find out they, like everyone else, are not good enough to get to heaven by being "something." Instead of being "something," they will find that they are "nothing."

Jesus said something else that day: "He who humbles himself will be exalted." *Show balloon.* When we come to God, asking for His help instead of thinking that we are too good to need Him, He fills us with His love and makes us "something"—His special children. *Blow up balloon.* That kind of being "something" is the only kind that lasts—forever and ever, as we live as God's chosen children in heaven.

Prayer: Lord, we come to You knowing that by ourselves we can never enter heaven. Thank You for sending Jesus to die for our sins. Help us always remember that it is only when You fill our lives with Your love that we are "something." Amen.

Follow Your Leader

———⟨◆⟩———

SIXTEENTH SUNDAY AFTER PENTECOST:
Luke 14:25–33

Text: "Anyone who does not carry his cross and follow Me cannot be My disciple." *Luke 14:27*

Teaching aids: Large and small cross, blindfold, small cross to give to each child.

Gospel truth: Jesus wants us to follow Him even when it is not easy.

All of us have played follow the leader. Can you tell me how it is done? *Let the children respond.* Someone is the leader who does things that everyone else has to copy.

Let's play follow the leader right now. See if you can do what I do. *Lead the children in seeing who can clap their hands, stamp their feet, and pat their heads. Then see who can snap their fingers or whistle—activities difficult for many young children to do.* Some of the things I did were easy for all of you to do. Some of the things were not so easy. It's not easy to play follow the leader when we have to do something hard.

Jesus is our leader in life. Can you think of ways in which following Jesus is easy? *Let the children respond.* Sometimes it's easy to be nice to others, to help them and say nice things to and about them. Sometimes it's easy to learn more about God and pray to Him.

Sometimes it's not so easy to follow Jesus. It may be hard to be nice to people who are not being nice to us. Someone may call us a name and we may want to call him or her a name back. Someone may play a mean trick on us and we may want to "get him back" with another mean trick. Praying for people who are mean to us may seem impossible to do.

When Jesus lived on earth, people were not always nice to Him. What did people who did not like Jesus finally do to Him? They put Him on a cross. People who did not believe that Jesus was God's Son were not always nice to Jesus' disciples either. Sometimes they put the disciples in jail for telling others about Jesus.

"Anyone who does not take up and carry his cross cannot follow Me," Jesus said to His disciples. *Show large cross.* What did Jesus do on a big cross for us? *Let the children respond.* He suffered and died for our sins. That's something we don't have to do to follow Jesus. Jesus did it once, for all time.

Because Jesus died on the big cross, He is there to help us as we try to live like Him today. Things that are hard to do the way Jesus wants us to are little crosses. Because Jesus died on the big cross, He is there to help us with the little crosses we have to face.

Show blindfold. There is another game I'd like to tell you about. This game is called a "trust walk." In it, someone is blindfolded and has to walk across a room. If I did that to you, how would you keep from running into something or falling down while you were blindfolded? *Let the children respond.* Having someone hold your hand and walk with you would make it easier to walk with a blindfold. The other person could look out for things that could get in your way and trip you. She could lead you away from places where you could get hurt.

Though we do not see Him, Jesus is always there by our side, guiding us as we follow Him, helping us through hard spots on our way. Follow Jesus, trust Jesus. He leads you with love to live forever with Him in heaven. Today I want to give you a little cross to take with you to your seats. Let it remind you to trust in Jesus to be with you as you follow Him through good and bad times today, and every day.

Prayer: Dear Jesus, it isn't always easy to follow You. Help us remember that whether it's easy or hard, You are always there by our side to guide us on our way. Amen.

Lost and Found

——▷◇◁——

SEVENTEENTH SUNDAY AFTER PENTECOST:
Luke 15:1–10

Text: Suppose one of you has a hundred sheep and loses one of them. Does he not leave the ninety-nine in the open country and go after the lost sheep until he finds it? *Luke 15:4–5*

Teaching aids: Stick puppets of little girl and her father, and a bowl of cotton balls. To make puppets, cut pictures from the advertising section of the Sunday paper and glue each one to a craft stick.

Gospel truth: God came to seek and to save all people.

Have you ever been lost? *Let the children respond.* Today I want to tell you a true story about a little girl named Michelle. Michelle was about two years old when this happened to her.

Use stick puppets to tell the story. Michelle liked to go out of the house by herself and look around. Several times she went down the street. Her parents did not want her to go out alone. They were afraid she would get hurt. They, and the rest of the children in Michelle's family, always tried to make sure the door was closed tightly when they went in and out of the house.

One day someone forgot and left the door open. Michelle saw it. She put on her red coat and went out into the cool winter evening. Nobody in her family saw her go.

Where is Michelle? wondered her father. He could not find her. He looked upstairs, downstairs, and in the basement. No Michelle. Then he found the open door and ran out to the front of the house. He got in his car and drove up the street. He drove down the street. There was no Michelle to be seen.

Michelle's father wandered around the backyard. He went back home and looked there. Still no Michelle. Michelle's father even climbed up to look in the tree house. From there he could see far away—to the street in back of their house. He looked and could not believe his eyes—there was Michelle in her red coat.

Michelle's father climbed down and ran to get Michelle. He carried her home, thanking God that his little girl was safe.

Hold up bowl of cotton balls. The story of Michelle reminds me of a story Jesus once told about a man who had one hundred sheep. That's a lot of sheep, isn't it? *Let the children respond.* You wouldn't think that one sheep out of so many would mean very much to the man, but it did.

One day, one little sheep trotted away on its own. *Drop cotton ball to floor.* The man left his other sheep to look for the lost sheep. He looked and looked until he found it. *Look around for the cotton ball, pretend to be happy to find it, and put it back in the bowl.*

The man picked up his sheep and carried it back on his shoulders. He was very happy that his sheep that had been lost was found. He was so happy that he had a big party to celebrate the sheep's return.

Sometimes people are like that little sheep. Michelle was like that sheep when she went out of the house and across the yard to another street where she shouldn't have gone. You and I wander away when we do other things that God does not want us to do.

What did the shepherd do when the sheep was lost? *Let the children respond.* He went looking for it. Just like Michelle's father started looking for her. Just like Jesus wants to bring us back to Him when we run away from Him by doing wrong things.

When the shepherd found the sheep, what did he do? *Let*

the children respond. He picked it up, put it on his shoulder, and took it home. Michelle's father picked her up and carried her home. And whatever we do, whatever bad thing we do that takes us away from Him, Jesus comes to us wherever we are, surrounding us with His forgiving love and taking us back into His family. We are never lost from God.

How does it make you feel to know that Jesus loves each of you so very much? *Let the children respond.* It gives you a warm feeling that makes you feel good inside, doesn't it? It's so good to know that Jesus is our Good Shepherd, always loving and taking care of us. Let's thank Jesus for His love right now.

Prayer: Dear Jesus, thank You for Your forgiving love. Thank You for being there to help us and forgive us when we have done wrong and to take us back into Your loving care. Amen.

Choose God

➤◆◀

EIGHTEENTH SUNDAY AFTER PENTECOST: Luke 16:1–13

Text: You cannot serve both God and Money. *Luke 16:13*

Teaching aid: Paper rectangle with dollar sign written on one side and the word *God* written on the other side.

Gospel truth: God, not money or the things it buys, should be most important in our life.

How many of you have played the game London Bridge? *Let the children respond.* How do you play it? *Let the children respond.* Two people stand with their hands together. *Demonstrate with two children.* Other children walk under the hands of the first two children as everyone sings: "London Bridge is falling down." *Demonstrate with several children.*

What happens after the song is finished? *Let the children respond.* The two children in the center put down their arms and "catch" a child. What happens next? *Let the children respond.* They have to choose between which of two things, such as ice cream or cake, that they like best. Then they stand beside the side they have chosen. When everyone has chosen, the two sides pull back to see which can pull the other across a center line.

London Bridge is just a game, but choosing between two things that both seem good is something we have to do every day. You had to make choices this morning, didn't you? What are some of them? *Let the children respond.* You may have chosen what shirt or dress to put on. You may have chosen what kind of cereal or roll to eat. Your parents made choices too. Deciding whether to sleep in or come to church was an important decision for them to make today.

We make choices all the time. Some of them, such as what color clothes to put on are not very important. Some of them, such as whether to come to hear God's Word or not, are very important.

One day, Jesus talked to some people who were listening to Him about an important choice they had to make. *Show paper rectangle.* The choice was between money or God. *Show paper with dollar sign on one side and then flip it over to show the side with God written on it.*

"You cannot serve both God and Money," Jesus said. At Jesus' time people served, or worked for, a master or boss. When Jesus said this, He meant that people had to decide what was most important in their life: God or money and the things it can buy.

Show the dollar sign. Working to earn a lot of money doesn't seem all bad. It can buy lots of things that make us happy. It can help us do things that are fun. We can even think of money as a gift from God.

The problem is when someone starts thinking that money, and what it buys, is the most important thing to work for in life. Why might someone want lots and lots of money? *Let the children respond.* Sometimes people think that if they can buy something, they will be happy. What might grownups want to buy to be happy? *Let the children respond.* Maybe a new car or some pretty clothes.

Sometimes children think all they need to be really happy is a special new toy. Have you ever thought that? *Let the children respond.* Maybe you wanted a new and bigger bike. Maybe a new doll. What happened after you got the new toy you had wanted so much and waited for so long? *Let the children respond.* Were you still so happy a few weeks later, or was there another new toy that you thought you needed to be really happy? *Let the children respond.* The problem with wanting things to make us happy is that there is always one more thing that we think we have to have to be really happy.

Jesus talked about people serving or working for either money or God. If all people do and think about is making more and more money, they don't have time to work for and think about God. They are doing what Jesus warned about, serving money not God.

Show the God side of the rectangle. Jesus said that people have to chose between money and God. What can God give us that money can't buy? *Let the children respond.* His love, His forgiveness, and a place in heaven. There we will be really happy, forever and ever. That kind of happiness money can't buy.

The Bible says that some people who heard Jesus that day liked money very much. They did not like what Jesus said that day. We have the same choice to make today: Do we make money or God the most important thing in our lives?

Remember when I said that today your families made a choice to come to church? That's the kind of choice that shows that God is the most important thing in the life of you and your family. Let's ask God to help us keep putting Him first in all we do the rest of the week.

At the start of our children's sermon we sang a song. Let's use that tune to sing a song that reminds us of the words of Jesus from our Gospel lesson today.

Let us serve the Lord, our God;
Lord, our God; Lord, our God.
Let us serve the Lord, our God.
Serve Him always.

Prayer: Lord, sometimes money and the things it can buy can seem more important than anything else in our lives. Help us remember that there is something even more important—You. Amen.

Take Time for God

———⋙◇⋘———

NINETEENTH SUNDAY AFTER PENTECOST: Luke 16:19–31

Text: Abraham replied, "They have Moses and the Prophets; let them listen to them." *Luke 16:29*

Teaching aids: Timer from a game; Bible with Acts l6:31 marked in it; paper plate with happy face on one side and sad face on the other. (*Note:* The travel game referred to in the text is called Perfection. Any other game with a timer may be substituted.)

Gospel truth: Take time for God before time is no more.

Show timer. Have any of you played a game that used a timer? *Let the children respond.* I have a travel game with little pieces that fit into holes on the playing board. To play the game you set the timer and see how many pieces you can put in during that time. What happens to the game when the timer goes off? *Let the children respond.* "Time's up!" we say. The game is over.

In team sports such as soccer or basketball, a time-keeper uses a timer to watch how long the game is to be played. What if, after your game is over, you realize that you and the other players on your side did something wrong that kept you from winning, and you want to go back and do it right? Can you do that? *Let the children respond.* No, it's too late. Your time is up.

When you play a game, it is important to do it right during the time you play. What helps you know how to play the game right? *Let the children respond.* Following directions written in a book or on the box helps in a board game. The coach helps you know how to play a team game the right way.

God has a time set for all of our lives on earth. Jesus once told a story about two men—the rich man and Lazarus—to remind us of this.

Show happy side of paper plate. The rich man in Jesus' story had a good life. He thought he had everything he needed. *Show sad side.* Lazarus, the poor man, stayed outside the rich man's house, begging for leftover food from the rich man's table. Dogs came and licked Lazarus' sores. The rich man did nothing to help.

Though Lazarus did not have many things like the rich man, he did have the one thing that was important when his time on earth was over. Do you know what that was? *Let the children respond.* Faith in God.

The day came for each man to die. *Show happy side.* Lazarus, who had faith in God, went to live with Him in heaven. There he sat in a place of honor and was comforted.

Show sad side. The rich man, who had lots of things but no faith, did not go to heaven. He went to hell. The rich man was not happy that he was not in heaven, but it was too late.

The rich man looked up and saw Lazarus beside Abraham. "Send Lazarus to help me," asked the rich man, but that could not be done.

"Send someone to warn my brothers," the rich man asked. "They already have God's Word," the rich man was told. "If they do not listen to that, not even someone coming from the dead will change them."

Show Bible. We too have the way to heaven given to us in the Bible. Do you know what it is? *Let the children respond. Then read Acts 16:31.* "Believe in the Lord Jesus, and you will be saved." That's the only way to heaven.

Like the rich man and Lazarus, God has a set time for us to live on earth. In God's Word we learn of the way to be ready for when our time is up. Let us take time to study

God's Word. Let us take time to pray, asking God for the saving faith that lasts forever.

Prayer: Lord, help us always be ready for the day when You call us to heaven. Help us use our time on earth to study Your Word and grow in our faith in You. Amen.

No Limit

TWENTIETH SUNDAY AFTER PENTECOST: Luke 17:1–10

Text: "If your brother sins, rebuke him, and if he repents, forgive him. If he sins against you seven times in a day, and seven times comes back to you and says, 'I repent,' forgive him." *Luke 17:3–4*

Teaching aid: White poster board rectangle, red marking pen, black marking pen, heart stickers (optional). Use a black marking pen to draw a black rectangle around the edge of each side of the poster board rectangle so both sides look like speed limit signs. On one side write **70** in the center; on the other side, write **No Limit**.

Gospel truth: Forgiveness has no limit.

Show 70 speed limit sign. Do you know what I have here? *Let the children respond.* It's a speed limit sign. You've all seen signs like this along the road. What number is on my sign? *Let the children respond.* Seventy. What does this number mean? *Let the children respond.* The 70 means that a driver cannot drive over 70 miles per hour on the part of the highway where this sign has been placed. The number on a speed limit sign limits, or stops, the driver from going any faster.

In our story today Jesus talks about whether there are any limits on how many times we forgive someone who asks us to forgive him or her.

Sometimes it's easy to forgive, and sometimes it's not so easy. What if someone steps on your toe by accident and says, "I'm sorry." Is it easy to forgive him? It's not too hard to forgive someone for something that was an accident.

What if another boy or girl says something to you that hurts you? He may make fun of you, or may say something bad about you to another child. Or, she may do something bad like take a toy that you're playing with, push you out of a line, or even hit you when she gets mad.

What if you tell someone who has been mean to you, "I don't like when you do that," and she says, "I'm sorry." Is it as easy to forgive as an accident? Why or why not? *Let the children respond.*

Jesus knew that it's not always easy for us to forgive each other. He talked to His disciples about forgiveness several times. Our Gospel reading today tells about one of those times. In it, Jesus tells His disciples that God wants them to forgive someone who asked their forgiveness not just once, but more.

Count to seven with me. Jesus said even if someone comes back and says, "I'm sorry," seven times in a day, we should forgive him or her. Seven is a lot of times to forgive in one day. What Jesus meant is that His friends should be ready to forgive not just once, but as many times as they were asked.

Show speed limit sign again. Another time Jesus said the disciples were to forgive seventy times seven times. That's the number written on this speed sign. Jesus used it to show that we should always be ready to forgive again and again.

Forgiving so many times seems hard to do—downright impossible, in fact. At least, the disciples seemed to think so. Do you know what they said when Jesus had said this to them? "Lord, increase our faith." They knew they couldn't forgive and forgive and forgive all by themselves. They needed more faith. Only with God's help could they forgive like God wanted them to.

It is the same for us today—only with God's help can we forgive each other like He wants us to. The disciples asked for more faith. That's what we need also—more faith in Jesus. *Use the red marking pen to draw a heart around the words "No Limit" on the poster board.* God's love for us has no limit. He is ready, for Jesus' sake, to forgive us when we turn to Him once, twice, seven, seventy, or even more times.

It is faith in this forgiving God that helps us forgive others—again and again. We forgive as we have been forgiven. Let's ask God for His help in forgiving right now.

Prayer: Lord, it's hard to forgive someone else not once, but again and again. Give us the faith we need to forgive others as You have forgiven us. In Jesus' name we pray. Amen.

Don't Forget to Say Thanks

TWENTY-FIRST SUNDAY AFTER PENTECOST:
Luke 17:11–19

Text: One of them, when he saw that he was healed, came back, praising God in a loud voice. He threw himself at Jesus' feet and thanked Him—and he was a Samaritan. *Luke 17:15–16*

Teaching aids: Large bow from a present

What is the most wonderful present you ever got? *Pass a gift-wrap bow around to the children as they tell of special gifts they have received.*

Ten men once got a special gift from Jesus. He healed them from a terrible skin disease that kept them from living with their families. Let me tell you the story from today's Gospel reading. As I do, use your hands to help me tell the story.

Ten men came to see Jesus.
Hold out ten fingers.
"Help us, Jesus!" the 10 men cried.
Hold your hands in pleading position.
Jesus made all 10 men well.
Show 10 fingers.
But only one man,
Hold up one finger
Remembered to thank Jesus.
Hold hands together, as in prayer.

Jesus has given you many gifts. Let's think of some of them. Our health, our families, a home, food, and clothes are some of them. Our toys and playmates are other gifts.

Look around the church today. Do you see anything that reminds you of other gifts God has given you? *Let the children respond.* What does the cross on the altar remind you of? *Let the children respond.* What does the baptismal font remind you of? *Let the children respond.* These are very special gifts of God that cure our sin-sickness.

What a lot we have to thank God for. Let's do so right now. After each part of the prayer that I say, answer with the words "Thank You, Lord."

For all the wonderful gifts you give us,
Thank You, Lord.
For food and drink,
Thank You, Lord.
For clothes and toys,
Thank You, Lord.
For house and school,
Thank You, Lord.
For life and health,
Thank You, Lord.
For family and friends,
Thank You, Lord.
For faith in You,
Thank You, Lord.
And for all else,
Thank You, Lord.
Amen.

Always on Call

TWENTY-SECOND SUNDAY AFTER PENTECOST:
Luke 18:1–8a

Text: And will not God bring about justice for His chosen ones, who cry out to Him day and night? Will He keep putting them off? I tell you, He will see that they get justice, and quickly. *Luke 18:7–8*

Teaching aids: Telephone (preferably with an answering machine built into it); two circle stick puppets. On one circle draw two eyes and a wavy line for a scowl. On the other circle draw two eyes and a short straight line for a mouth. Glue both circle faces to craft sticks.

Gospel truth: God hears and answers the prayers of His children.

Show telephone. When we call our friends or relatives, they may have different ways of answering the phone. What may happen when you dial a number? *Let the children respond.* You may get an answering machine that asks you to leave a message. Some people have an answering machine that keeps a record of the numbers and names of people who call them—with a recording that says they will call back later. Some people have a list of numbers that you listen to and then punch into the telephone before you can leave a message for someone to call you back.

What if you really needed to talk to the person you were calling right away? How would you feel about getting the answering machine? *Let the children respond.* You might feel like you will never get through to the person you need to talk to right away.

Sometimes when we call someone, he or she gets another call and we get put on hold. We might wait and wait and wait for the person to get back to us. Sometimes the person we had been talking to forgets about us. We wait and wait and they don't come back to talk to us at all. How do you feel when you wait and wait, all for nothing? *Let the children respond.* You may feel like you will never get to tell the other person what you wanted to tell him or her.

Hold a stick puppet in each hand as you tell the story. Jesus told a story once to show how we should not give up when we try to talk to God. It's a story about a bad judge and a widow, a woman whose husband had died.

Do you know what a judge does? *Let the children respond.* Sometimes people have an argument that they can't work out by themselves. It might be about property. It might be about who did the wrong thing when someone gets hurt. A judge listens to the story about what happened and decides the fair thing to do, like your mother does when you and your brother or sister can't work out an argument.

The judge in Jesus' story was not a good judge. He did not believe in God or care about people. He did not care about justice, another word for fairness. A widow kept coming to this bad judge. "Give me justice!" she kept asking. "Protect me from the person who is trying to hurt me."

For a long time the judge did not listen to the woman. Did she give up? No, she didn't. The woman kept coming back to the judge again and again. Finally he gave up and said, "I don't care about God, and I don't care about what people think, but I'll give this woman what she wants just to stop her from bothering me."

The bad judge saw that the woman was finally treated fairly. How much more, Jesus said, does God see that His children who cry to Him for help day and night are treated fairly. God will see that their cries for help are quickly answered.

Hold telephone. Remember when we talked about how hard it is sometimes to try to talk to someone on the telephone? Sometimes it is hard to get through to the person we want to talk to. That's not the way it is when we try to talk to God.

What happens when you pray to God? *Let the children respond.* He hears us right away. He never makes it hard to get through to Him. He never waits until later to listen to us. He never puts us off to listen to someone else first. When we want to talk to God, He is there—listening with love to whatever we want to say.

The judge in the story took a long time to help the woman with her problem. That's not how God is. God is there to help us right when we need it, in the way that is best for us.

God is a good judge, seeing that His children are treated fairly. Have faith. Believe that God can and will help you. Trust Him to be there in all your needs.

Prayer: Lord, give us faith to come to You with all our problems, both big and little. Thank You for being there to hear and answer us in all our needs. Amen.

No Copies Allowed

━━▶◆◀━━

THIRD-LAST SUNDAY IN THE CHURCH YEAR:
Luke 21:5–19

Text: He replied, "Watch out that you are not deceived. For many will come in My name, claiming, 'I am he,' and 'The time is near.' Do not follow them." *Luke 21:8*

Teaching aids: Picture of Jesus, with two photocopies, one darker and one lighter than the original; paper cross placed in a Bible. Mount the pictures on poster board. Label them A, B, and C, with picture B being the original.

Gospel truth: There is only one Jesus, the Jesus of the Bible.

Have you ever copied a picture on a photocopy machine? Is the picture you copied always the same as the first picture? *Let the children respond.* Usually, unless you have the setting just right, the copies do not look the same. This morning I brought several pictures of Jesus. One is the original picture, the other two are copies. Let's look at them. *Show pictures.* How are the pictures alike? *Let the children respond.* How are the pictures different? *Let the children respond.*

Let's vote on which picture you think is the original. Raise your hand if you think it is picture A. *Let the children respond.* Picture B. *Let the children respond.* Picture C. *Let the children respond.* Those who chose picture B are right. This is the original picture. *Point to original picture.* One picture is a lighter copy, and one picture is a darker copy.

Only one picture is the right one.

Do you know what a "wanna-be" is? It's someone who wants to be like someone else. The "wanna-be" may even try to dress and act like the person he wants to be like, but it isn't the same.

In today's Bible reading, Jesus warns His disciples to watch out for people who would come after He was gone saying that they were the real Jesus, the special promised one of God. The people Jesus warned about would be "wanna-bes" who seem like they might be Jesus but aren't at all. These Jesus "wanna-bes" may look and act like people think Jesus should look and act, but they aren't the real thing. They are only bad copies.

Throughout the years since Jesus went back to heaven, people have tried to say that they were the real Jesus come back to earth. Sometimes they even tried to add to God's Word, telling a new way to be saved instead of through faith in Jesus.

How do we know the real Jesus? *Let the children respond. Then show Bible and take out cross.* The real Jesus is the Jesus of the Bible. By reading the Bible, we learn how Jesus was the promised one of God. What does the Bible tell us about Jesus? It tells us that the real Jesus came to earth on the first Christmas. That He died on the cross for our sins and rose again on Easter. *Show cross.* He ascended into heaven and will come again on the Last Day to take us to live with Him forever in heaven. Though we do not see Him, He is always with us to hear and help us.

That's the Jesus of the Bible. That's the Jesus we should follow, not a copy, or a "wanna be" Jesus, that tells us otherwise.

Prayer: Lord, help us to look to the Bible to find You, the real promised one of God that is the way to heaven. Amen.

A Gift that Keeps on Giving

SECOND-LAST SUNDAY IN THE CHURCH YEAR:
Luke 19:11–27

Text: "So he called ten of his servants and gave them ten minas. 'Put this money to work,' he said, 'until I come back.'" *Luke 19:13*

Teaching aids: Cardboard box covered with wrapping paper; gift bow attached to box lid; paper heart with a cross on it placed inside the box. Prepare box so that the top can either be lifted off or is a flap easily opened.

Gospel truth: God gives gifts to be used.

Today I brought a present. We all like to get presents. What kind of gift do you like to get? *Let the children respond.* What do you like to do with your gifts when you get them? *Let the children respond.* You like to use them right away, don't you?

Jesus told a story about a master, or boss, who gave money to his workers. Then he went away to a far away country. The workers did not all do the same thing with their money. Some used their money to make more money. Their gifts grew and grew.

One man did not use the money he had been given. He hid it instead, and it stayed just the same.

When the master came back, he asked each of the workers how they had used their gift from him. How do you think the master felt about the workers who had used his gifts wisely? *Let the children respond.* He was very happy with them. How do you think the master felt about the worker who had hidden his gift and not done anything at all with it? *Let the children respond.* The master was not happy at all. He took away the gift and gave it to the man who had done the most with his gift.

Earlier we talked about different gifts that other people have given us. What about special gifts from God? Can you think of what those gifts might be? *Let the children respond.* God has given you different things to do well. Let's see if you can take turns telling what special things God helps some of you do. Who can sing well? jump well? tell funny jokes? run fast? read well? *Let the children respond.* I bet if we went on, we would find that there is a special gift from God that each of you has. These are all special gifts that God wants you to use for Him, not hide away.

Do you know what the most important gift of God to you is? *Open box lid and take out the heart with the cross drawn on it.* It is the gift of faith in Jesus as your Savior. That's a gift for all time. That's the best gift of all.

How can you help this faith in Jesus grow in other people? *Let the children respond.* Can you think of someone who needs to know more about Jesus? What can you say or do to help him or her know more about Jesus? *Let the children respond.* Helping someone else come to faith in Jesus is one of the most wonderful ways we can use the gifts God has given us.

Prayer: Lord, thank You for the many special gifts You have given us. Thank You especially for the gift of faith. Help us show our love for You by using these gifts to share Your love with others. Amen.

Ready Workers

LAST SUNDAY IN THE CHURCH YEAR:
Luke 12:42–48

Text: The Lord answered, "Who then is the faithful and wise manager, whom the master puts in charge of his servants to give them their food allowance at the proper time? It will be good for that servant whom the master finds doing so when he returns." *Luke 12:42–43*

Teaching aids: Lawn rake and Bible.

Gospel truth: Jesus wants to find faithful workers when He returns on the Last Day.

Do your ever have special jobs to do for your parents? *Let the children respond. Hold up rake.* Perhaps they asked you to rake the leaves for them this fall. Maybe your mother or father asked you to rake the leaves into a pile, then they left to work on another part of the yard.

What if, instead of working the whole time, you played in the pile of leaves you made? If your parents came back and found you playing, what might they say? *Let the children respond.* They might ask why you are not doing the job they left you to do.

Jesus told a story about a man whose master left him with a big job to do—he was to take care of his master's other servants by giving them their food. What do you think the master would expect to find when he came back home? *Let the children respond.* The man should be doing his job.

If the man was taking good care of the other servants, what do you think he would get? *Let the children respond.* Maybe he would get a reward. If he was not doing his job, what do you think would happen to him? *Let the children respond.* Yes, he might be sent away.

Jesus told this story to His disciples. After Jesus went back to heaven, the disciples would have a big job to do for Jesus on earth. The man in the story had a big job to do in giving the other workers their food. The disciples were given the big job of giving other people the Good News of Jesus and His saving love for them.

Who are Jesus' disciples today? *Let the children respond.* You and I are Jesus' disciples. God gives us a job to do too. What job do you and I have to do for God today? *Let the children respond.* He wants us to share the Good News of Jesus and His love with others. *Show Bible and rake.* We use a rake to gather together leaves. God wants us to use His Word to bring others to faith in Jesus.

What an important job God has given us—the most important job there can be. God wants us to share the story of Jesus and His love with others. What are some things you can do to share Jesus love? *Let the children respond.* What can you say to share Jesus' love? *Let the children respond.*

Jesus will come again. We don't know when—only God knows that. What we do know is that when Jesus comes, He wants to find us doing His work, sharing the story of His forgiving love with others. Let us ask God to help us always be willing workers for Him, always ready for the day when He comes back to take all who believe in Him to live with Him in heaven.

Prayer: Dear Lord, thank You for letting us share with Your work on earth. Help us joyfully share the Good News of Your life and death on the cross. Let us always be ready for the day when You come back to earth. Amen.